King Charles III started his reign with a determined effort to meet ordinary people across the United Kingdom's four nations. (MOD/Crown Copyright)

CONTENTS

Queen Elizabeth II's funeral last September saw huge numbers of people participate in events to allow them to show their respects. (MOD/Crown Copyright)

The late Queen's last ever Buckingham Palace balcony appearance marked the passing of generations in the royal family. (MOD/Crown Copyright)

London was at the centre of State Funeral for Queen Elizabeth II. (MOD/Crown Copyright)

Cover image: MOD/Crown Copyright

Charles, as Prince of Wales, at the COP21 climate conference. Tackling climate change has been one of The King's enduring passions. (Arnaud Bouissou)

KING CHARLES

The Making of Britain's Monarch

On May 6, 2023 King Charles III will be crowned in Westminster Abbey and London will be packed with hundreds of thousands of visitors celebrating the happy event. Around the country and the Commonwealth, The King's coronation will, no doubt, be celebrated in considerable style.

It is nearly 70 years since Britain last celebrated the coronation of a new monarch so it is going to be a new experience for the majority of the nation's population.

In *King Charles III: The Making of Britain's*

Monarch, we look forward to the big day and give an idea of the events taking place in London and further afield. We also look at the history of coronations and explain what the ceremonial aspects mean, as well as explaining how the service has evolved over the centuries. The coronation of King Charles III is expected to incorporate many new features that have been developed out of the age old traditions for this highly symbolic royal event.

We also tell the story of The King's life over the past 73 years and look in detail at his accession to the throne last September.

The life and times of King Charles III span

from the days of post-World War Two Britain in the late 1940s when rationing was still in force, the sun still did not set on the British Empire and most homes were heated by coal fires.

The then Prince of Wales came of age in the late 1960s, when Britain's capital was known as 'swinging London'. This was the age of flower power, the Beatles, and Carnaby Street boutiques.

In the 1970s, he served in the armed forces and captained a Royal Navy mine sweeper, while at the same time living with the tag of being 'the Western world's most eligible bachelor'.

The King has spent a lifetime in uniform and has a strong affinity with the men and women of Britain's armed forces. (@RoyalFamily)

Royal Fly Past. Queen Elizabeth and the royal family on the Buckingham Palace balcony during the Platinum Jubilee fly past. (MOD/Crown Copyright)

The King is very engaged with government ministers and political leaders of all hues. Here he meets Chris Heaton-Harris, the Secretary of State for Northern Ireland. (@Royal Family)

III

ISBN: 978 1 80282 638 8
Editor: Tim Ripley
Senior editor, specials: Roger Mortimer
Email: roger.mortimer@keypublishing.com
Design: Dan Hilliard
Advertising Sales Manager: Brodie Baxter
Email: brodie.baxter@keypublishing.com
Tel: 01780 755131
Advertising Production: Debi McGowan
Email: debi.mcgowan@keypublishing.com

SUBSCRIPTION/MAIL ORDER
Key Publishing Ltd, PO Box 300, Stamford, Lincs, PE9 1NA Tel: 01780 480404
Subscriptions email: subs@keypublishing.com
Mail Order email: orders@keypublishing.com
Website: www.keypublishing.com/shop

PUBLISHING
Group CEO: Adrian Cox
Publisher, Books and Bookazines: Jonathan Jackson

Published by
Key Publishing Ltd, PO Box 100, Stamford, Lincs, PE9 1XQ
Tel: 01780 755131
Website: www.keypublishing.com

PRINTING
Precision Colour Printing Ltd, Haldane, Halesfield 1, Telford, Shropshire. TF7 4QQ

DISTRIBUTION
Seymour Distribution Ltd, 2 Poultry Avenue, London, EC1A 9PU
Enquiries Line: 02074 294000.

PHOTO CREDITS: The authors have attempted where possible to trace the copyright holders of all the images. Any errors will be corrected in future editions.

His world changed after the fairytale wedding to Diana, Princess of Wales in 1981 and the arrival of his two sons, Princes William, and Harry. However, this was also the start of King Charles III's interest in conservation of the environment and the establishment the Princes' Trust to help disadvantaged young people.

The 1990s were a tumultuous time for the future King as his marriage ran into trouble and several scandals dominated media coverage of the royal family.

However, a new century brought stability to King Charles III's life and his second marriage to Camilla, now Queen Consort.

As his mother and father's health began to deteriorate, he was called on to carry out more royal duties and become increasingly involved in affairs of state. The past decade has seen many of his concerns about the environment go mainstream, resulting in him representing the British government at official events to confront the challenges of climate change.

The passing of his mother last September set off a chain of ceremonial events to smooth the new King's accession to the throne. His conduct during those momentous 10 days won King Charles III much good will and set his new reign off to flying start.

We hope you enjoy *King Charles III: The Making of Britain's Monarch* and it helps you better understand Britain's royals, the pomp and ceremony that has survived for generations, and the events over the coronation weekend. It promises to be an enjoyable and memorable time.

Hopefully, our publication will also be a lasting and treasured memento of this important and historic milestone in British life.

Happy royal reading ●

Tim Ripley Editor

Cheering crowds are expected to line roads across London during the Coronation. (MOD/Crown Copyright)

A NEW KING IS CROWNED

What to expect during the Coronation Weekend

Three days of celebrations are planned for May 2023 to mark the coronation of King Charles III, which will see him make his first appearance on the Buckingham Palace balcony as monarch. The service will also see the coronation of the Queen Consort, Camilla. With the coronation service itself taking place on a Saturday, communities the length and breadth of the United Kingdom and Commonwealth will be celebrating the event, but the UK government has also announced that the following Monday – May 8 - will be a bank holiday for England, Northern Ireland, Scotland, and Wales.

Details of the Coronation Weekend were released by Buckingham Palace in January and preparations are now well underway for what promises to be a historic and memorable occasion.

The weekend will kick off with The King's coronation in Westminster Abbey on Saturday May 6 and continue through to the Monday when UK schools and most work places will be closed.

The Archbishop of Canterbury, Justin Welby will conduct the service and Buckingham Palace said it "will reflect the Monarch's role today and look towards the future, while being rooted in longstanding traditions and pageantry. Across the Coronation Weekend, there will be further opportunities for people to come together in celebration of the historic occasion."

Buckingham Palace said that The King and Queen Consort "hope the Coronation Weekend will provide an opportunity to spend time and celebrate with friends, families and communities across the United Kingdom, the Realms, and the Commonwealth. [The royal couple] are looking forward to marking the occasion with the public throughout 2023."

Saturday May 6

The Coronation Service will take place on the morning of May 6, which Buckingham Palace describe as "a solemn religious service, as well as an occasion for celebration and pageantry."

It will start with the arrival of The King and his wife at Westminster Abbey in procession from Buckingham Palace, known as 'The

King's Procession'.

The service is set to be considerably shorter than the coronation of his mother in 1953 - which ran for more than three hours - with several elements reduced or dispensed with. However, royal traditionalists will not be entirely disappointed because key elements of the 900 year old service are retained, including the placing of St Edward's Crown – the traditional centrepiece of the Crown Jewels - on The King's head and then he will be anointed as monarch by the Archbishop of Canterbury. The Queen Consort, Camilla will also be crowned and Prince William will be formally confirmed as Prince of Wales. Although VIP guests from around the world have been invited to attend, the size of the guest list has been dramatically scaled back compared to 1953 when 8,000 people were crammed into the Abbey. Only some 2,000 official guests are to attend in May.

After the service, The King will return to Buckingham Palace in a larger ceremonial procession, known as 'The Coronation Procession'. The royal couple will be joined in this procession by other members of the royal family.

At Buckingham Palace, The King, accompanied by other members of his family, will appear to make his first appearance on its iconic balcony as monarch to conclude the day's ceremonial events.

Hundreds of thousands of visitors are expected to travel to the capital, so the public are advised to arrive early. For those unable to attend, the event will be televised and live cast on the internet leading to expectations of a multi-million strong global audience.

Sunday, May 7

A special Coronation Concert will be staged at Windsor Castle and broadcast live by the BBC with 10,000 tickets having been distributed via public ballot. The ballot closed on February 28 but the event, which will be produced by BBC Studios, is being broadcast live on BBC One, ➲

A flypast by the RAF Battle of Britain Memorial Flight is expected to feature during the Coronation Weekend. (MOD/Crown Copyright)

Buckingham Palace will be the focus of public celebrations with the new King expected to make his first iconic balcony appearance. (MOD/Crown Copyright)

BBC iPlayer, BBC Radio 2, and BBC Sounds.

The star studded event will bring global music icons and contemporary stars together in celebration of the historic occasion, said Buckingham Palace.

Attended by a public audience including volunteers from The King and Queen Consort's many charity affiliations, the concert will see a world-class orchestra play interpretations of musical favourites fronted by some of the world's biggest entertainers, alongside performers from the world of dance. The performances will be supported by staging and effects located on the Castle's East Lawn and will also feature a selection of spoken word sequences delivered by stars of stage and screen.

Alongside the stars of the concert, the show will also see an exclusive appearance from the Coronation Choir. This diverse group will be created from the nation's keenest community choirs and amateur singers from across the United Kingdom, such as refugee choirs, NHS choirs, LGBTQ+ singing groups and deaf signing choirs.

A new documentary exploring the formation of the choirs will tell the stories of the people representing the many faces and voices of the country.

The Coronation Choir will appear alongside the Virtual Choir, made up of singers from across the Commonwealth, for a special performance on the night.

> **"Coronation Big Lunch brings the celebrations to your neighbourhood and is a great way to get to know your community a little better"**

Justin Welby, The Archbishop of Canterbury, will preside over King Charles III's coronation. (Roger Harris, UK Parliament)

The centrepiece of the Coronation Concert, 'Lighting up the Nation', will see the country join together in celebration as iconic locations across the United Kingdom are lit up using projections, lasers, drone displays and illuminations.

The Coronation Big Lunch

Neighbours and communities across the United Kingdom have been invited by The King and Queen Consort to share food and fun together at Coronation Big Lunches, in a nationwide act of celebration and friendship. "From a cup of tea with a neighbour to a street party, a Coronation Big Lunch brings the celebrations to your neighbourhood and is a great way to get to know your community a little better," said Buckingham Palace.

The Coronation Big Lunch will be overseen and organised by the Big Lunch team at the Eden Project in Cornwall. The Big Lunch is an idea from the Eden Project, made possible by The National Lottery, that brings millions of people together annually to boost community spirit, reduce loneliness and support charities and good causes. The Queen Consort has been Patron of the Big Lunch since 2013.

Free downloadable resources will also be made available online by the Big Lunch team at CoronationBigLunch.com, to help people and communities with their Coronation Big Lunch planning.

Westminster Abbey in the heart of London will be at the centre of national celebrations to mark the coronation of King Charles III. (Rabanus Flavus)

The Gold State Coach has carried every British Monarch to their coronation since George IV in 1821. (MOD/Crown Copyright)

Red coated Guardsmen from every regiment in the Household Division will have a prominent role in the coronation. (MOD/Crown Copyright)

King Charles III will be out and about around London during the coronation weekend in May. (MOD/Crown Copyright)

Monday, May 8

On the new UK bank holiday, members of the public will be invited by The King to take part in the Big Help Out, encouraging people to join the work being undertaken to support their local areas.

The Big Help Out is being organised by the Together Coalition and a wide range of partners, such as the Scouts, the Royal Voluntary Service and faith groups from across the country. "The Big Help Out will highlight the positive impact volunteering has on communities across the nation," said Buckingham Palace. "In tribute to The King's public service, the Big Help Out will encourage people to try volunteering for themselves and join the work being undertaken to support their local areas. The aim of the Big Help Out is to use volunteering to bring communities together and create a lasting volunteering legacy from the Coronation Weekend." ●

The troopers of the Household Cavalry's Mounted Regiment will escort King Charles III and other members of the royal family around London during the Coronation Weekend. (MOD/Crown Copyright)

HISTORIC KINGS

Britain's Monarchy

Britain's monarchy stretches back more than a thousand years and apart from a short period in the 17th century it has been one of the few constants in the history of the British Isles.

King Charles III is the latest monarch to reign over the United Kingdom and his family tree has roots in England, Scotland, and Ireland. There are mythical British monarchs stretching back to the Roman occupation, with the most famous being Arthur, who according to legend had a round table.

Historical evidence exists for British monarchs in the 9th century, and it is in this period that the bloodlines for King Charles III start. Earliest kings on the British Isles were recorded in Pictish kingdoms in Scotland and Ireland. At the same time the first Wessex monarch, King Alfred was ruling in southwest England

Over the following centuries the royal lines in England and Scotland became intertwined. The rival royal houses inter-married and then fought each other. The arrival of the Normans under William the Conqueror in 1066 broke the rule

> **"Britain's role in the world has also been transformed over the past 70 years with the demise of the British Empire"**

of Anglo-Saxon English monarchs, opening the way for the medieval monarchs of the Houses of York, Lancaster, and Tudor. When the warrior queen, Elizabeth I died without a direct heir, the English crown passed to James of Scotland in 1603, who united the monarchies of Scotland and England for the first time.

The thrones of England and Scotland were temporarily vacant for eleven years after Charles I was executed in 1649 and Oliver Cromwell set up Britain's only ever republic or Commonwealth, as he called it.

The House of Stuart (originally spelled Stewart) rule came to end when Queen Anne died childless in 1714 and Britain turned to Germany for her cousin, George I, to ensure the throne passed to a protestant. King George's line reigned until Victoria took the throne in 1837. Her marriage to Prince Albert saw the British royal family renamed the House of Saxe-Coburg and Gotha and increased its linkages to several monarchies across Europe. During the Victorian era and then the Edwardian period after the turn of the 20th century, these royal connections

Queen Elizabeth II of the House of Windsor was Britain's longest serving monarch. (NFB Canada)

AND QUEENS

George V and Queen Mary arrived in Delhi at the peak of the British Empire before World War One. He was the first monarch of the House of Windsor. (Imperial War Museum)

were not controversial.

The turmoil of World War One caused massive upheavals in British society and this unleashed forces that not even the royal family could contain. Britain was now at war with Germany and the Austro-Hungarian Empire so the royal family had to make concerted efforts to distance themselves from many of their European relatives who were ruling over countries that were fighting Britain and her allies. When Russia was engulfed in revolution in 1917 and its absolute monarchy overthrown the British royal family looked increasingly out of touch with public opinion. So, King George V decided that a new start was needed and changed the family name to the more British sounding Windsor.

George V's surefooted reign and leadership during World War One cemented the House of Windsor's place in British life for the following century. There was a brief hiccup in 1936, when Edward VIII abdicated after a reign of just 326 days and was succeeded by his younger brother, King George VI. King's Charles III's granddad reigned for 16 years and then his mother, Queen Elizabeth II, ascended to the throne. King George VI only had daughters, so for his reign his heir could not assume the traditional title of Prince of Wales.

In the span of history, British Kings and Queens have gone from being absolute monarchs who ruled by divine right to constitutional monarchs, who have a ceremonial role in Britain's parliamentary democracy. Britain's role in the world has also been transformed over the past 70 years with the demise of the British Empire. British society has undergone profound changes. King George V recognised that the royal family needed to keep on the right side of public opinion in times of turmoil and since then, his heirs have recognised that they only reign with the consent of their subjects. ●

The Victoria Memorial in front of Buckingham Palace was built to commemorate her 63 year long reign. (MOD/Crown Copyright)

Queen Elizabeth's marriage to Philip Mountbatten in November 1947 secured the future of the House of Windsor. (Nederlands Fotocollectie Anefo)

The crowning of Queen Elizabeth II on June 2, 1953, was the first British coronation of the modern media era. (Corbis Hulton Deutsch Getty)

CROWNING A MONARCH

What Happens During a Coronation

Crowning a monarch is more complicated than just putting a crown on their head. It is meant to symbolise the formal transition from one monarch to another, with the focus on celebrating the new monarch's upcoming reign.

The modern British service of coronation can trace its origins back to 973AD and the coronation of King Edgar in Bath, but it has been constantly evolving. Every monarch wants to put their personal stamp on the proceedings to put their mark on history. Given that they only get crowned once in their lives, this is not really surprising.

In the days when Britain's monarchs were absolute rulers this was a way for them to shape their ruling regime and its grip on power. Nobles who pledged allegiance actually controlled armies and bands of knights who the king depended on to put down peasant revolts or fight foreign wars. In modern times, the coronation has become a largely symbolic event to mark the transition of monarchs. It is also seen as a major boost to tourism and an opportunity for government ministers and officials to interact with senior foreign VIP guests. It is British soft power in action.

Since 1066 the coronation has been held in Westminster Abbey, although previous coronations were recorded in Bath, Oxford, Canterbury, and Winchester. After the Union of Crowns, coronations would take place in both England and Scotland but the practice was discontinued in 1685 by James VII. Since then Scottish nobles were invited to attend the coronation ceremony in London.

While the essential elements of the coronation have remained largely unchanged for the past thousand years, no two coronations are the same. The monarch is first presented to, and acclaimed by, the people. He then swears an oath to uphold the law and the Church. Following that, the monarch is anointed with holy oil, invested with regalia, and

crowned, before receiving the homage of their subjects. Consorts of Kings are then anointed and crowned as Queens. The service ends with a closing procession and since the 20th century it has been traditional for the royal family to appear later on the balcony of Buckingham Palace before attending a banquet there.

As the last coronation that anyone alive can remember took place in June 1953, it inevitably gets held up as the benchmark of coronations. It in turn had been based on Queen Elizabeth II's father's coronation in 1937, which she herself attended as an 11 year old and must have vividly remembered.

The scale of Queen Elizabeth II's coronation was unprecedented, 30,000 military personnel joined the royal procession or lined the routes to and from Westminster Abbey and 7,000 police officers provided security.

The service started with Queen Elizabeth II entering Westminster Abbey behind the St Edward's Crown, which was carried into the Abbey by the Lord High Steward of England, who was flanked by two other peers. A trio of bishops greeted the young monarch at the entrance to the abbey and her procession then moved into the heart of the ancient building, followed by the high commissioners of the Commonwealth carrying banners bearing the shields of the coats of ➲

Celebrations for Queen Elizabeth II's coronation took place around the Commonwealth. (PD Australia)

The official coronation portrait of Queen Elizabeth II and her husband radiated regal authority. She reigned over the transformation of Britain from a global empire into a modern multi-cultural country. (Canadian National Archives)

Crowds filled the streets of central London to watch Queen Elizabeth II travel back and forth from Westminster Abbey. (Empics PA/Alamy)

Queen Elizabeth II's husband, Philip masterminded the open access of the media to his wife's coronation, which included live television coverage for the first time. (Getty/Hulton Archive)

arms of their respective nations.

As Queen Elizabeth II prayed at and then seated herself on the Chair of Estate to the south of the altar, the bishops carried in the religious paraphernalia—the Bible, paten and chalice.

Seated on the Chair of Estate, Queen Elizabeth II then took the Coronation Oath as administered by the Archbishop of Canterbury. In the lengthy oath, she swore to govern each of her countries according to their respective laws and customs, to mete out law and justice with mercy, to uphold Protestantism in the United Kingdom and protect the Church of England, as well as preserving its bishops and clergy. She proceeded to the altar where she stated, "The things which I have here promised, I will perform, and keep. So help me God", before kissing the Bible and putting the royal sign-manual to the oath as the Bible was returned to the Dean of Westminster. From him the moderator of the General Assembly of the Church of Scotland, took the Bible and

presented it to Queen Elizabeth II again.

The communion service was then conducted, involving prayers by both the clergy and Queen Elizabeth II. She was then anointed monarch as she sat in King Edward's Chair. This is the most symbolic event of the ceremony and involved the Archbishop of Canterbury, assisted by the Dean of Westminster. The archbishop made a cross on her forehead, hands and breast with holy oil

> ## "Charles was the first child who is known to have witnessed his mother's coronation as monarch"

made from the same base as had been used in the coronation of her father. At her request, the anointing ceremony was the only party of the proceedings not televised or photographed.

Next, came the investiture, with various royal regalia and accoutrements being handed to new monarch for her to wear or hold. These included the Sword of State, the Armills (bracelets), Stole Royal, Robe Royal and the Sovereign's Orb, followed by the Queen's Ring, the Sovereign's Sceptre with Cross and the Sovereign's Sceptre with Dove. Queen Elizabeth II was then crowned by the archbishop, with the crowd chanting "God save the Queen!" three times at the exact moment St Edward's Crown touched the monarch's head. The princes and peers present then put on their coronets and a 21-gun salute was fired from the Tower of London. Prince Philip then swore allegiance to his wife, rather than be crowned King.

It was now the turn of the assembled princes, bishops and peers to pay their personal homage

King George VI was crowned in May 1937, and he was on the throne throughout World War Two. (Rijksmuseum)

and allegiance. Queen Elizabeth II then removed all her royal regalia; she knelt and took the communion. Now wearing the Imperial State Crown and holding the Sceptre with the Cross and the Orb, and as the gathered guests sang "God Save the Queen", the new monarch left Westminster Abbey through the nave and apse, out the Great West Door.

The return route to Buckingham Palace was designed so that the procession could be seen by as many people in London as possible. The 7.2km route took the 16,000 participants two hours to complete. Many people camped in The Mall to catch a glimpse of the procession, including a family who had sailed all the way from Australia in a ketch for the occasion. Thousands more celebrated throughout the country and the Commonwealth with street parties.

The coronation of 1953 was ground-breaking in its own right, with the ceremony including many firsts. A representative of a Church other

Children gather in Parliament Square in May 1937 to watch the rehearsal of the Coronation of George VI. (Leonard Bentley)

than the Church of England, the Moderator of the Church of Scotland, took part for first time since the reformation. The British monarch is not formally head of the Church of Scotland but is duty bound by the 1707 Act of Union to uphold the Protestant religion. Prince Charles was the first child who is known to have witnessed his mother's coronation as monarch.

It was the first ever to be televised, it was watched by 27 million people in the UK alone - out of a total population of 36 million people - and millions more in audiences around the world. Another 11 million listened on the radio in Britain. BBC coverage of the coronation was a breakthrough for the history of broadcasting. The live broadcasting of the ceremony was controversial and it subsequently emerged that the royal and Church authorities had not wanted live coverage. Only the intervention of the monarch, at the prompting of her husband, overcame this resistance to the royal family entering the modern media era. ●

A ROYAL CHILDHOOD

Young Prince Charles

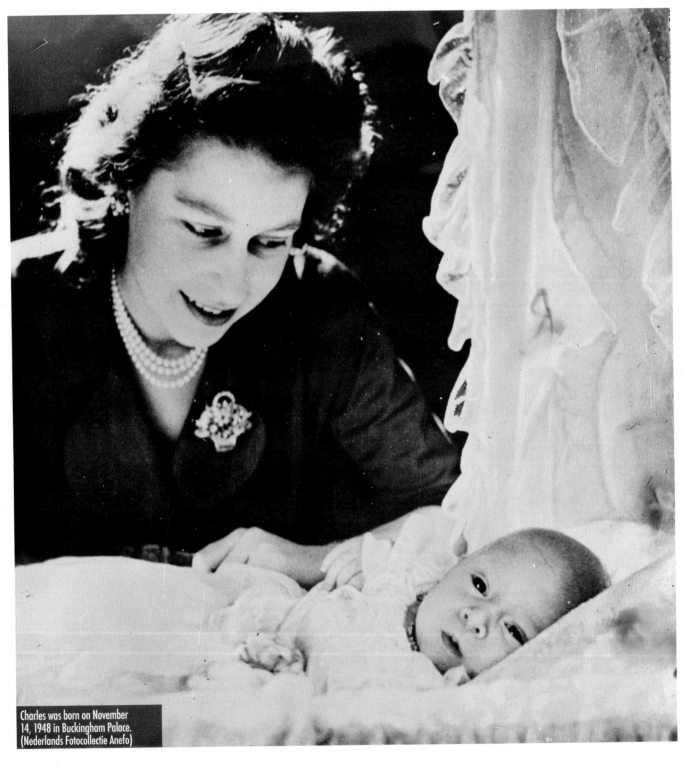

Charles was born on November 14, 1948 in Buckingham Palace. (Nederlands Fotocollectie Anefo)

In 1950, Charles was joined by his sister, Anne, and the young royals soon started to take part in public events. (Archive and Library of Canada)

Charles Philip Arthur George was born at Buckingham Palace on November 14, 1948. With his mother's accession to the throne in February 1952, Prince Charles, at the age of three, became heir apparent or second-in-line of succession. From this point on his life centred around preparing to be King one day.

If he had not immediately realised what was in store for him, after attending his mother's coronation in Westminster Abbey he would have seen for himself that his mother had a unique and extraordinary job. His role as heir apparent was formally recognised in 1958 when he was appointed Prince of Wales.

Unlike his mother, who had spent much of her childhood not expecting to become monarch, Charles could never escape his royal destiny. His early years involved activities designed by his parents to prepare him for his royal duties and

only once an adult could he progressively follow his own interests.

The young prince's upbringing was very different from that experienced by his mother. Like many other children of aristocrats of that era, the young Princess Elizabeth was educated

> ## "Unlike his mother, who had spent much of her childhood not expecting to become monarch, Charles could never escape his royal destiny."

entirely at home by nannies and governesses. During her long reign, Queen Elizabeth II probably opened more schools, colleges, universities and educational institutions that anyone else on the planet but she never spent a single day at school himself.

The young Prince Charles followed a very different path. His father's troubled upbringing meant he had never experienced a life of luxury and was convinced of the value of 'character forming' experiences for his son.

After turning five, he was educated at Buckingham Palace with his sister by a governess, Catherine Peebles. However, when he turned eight, his education started to take a very different path and the young prince was enrolled at Hill House school in West London. This was a revolution in royal education, making him the first heir apparent to attend school. He joined in school sports and other activities with the other boys. His parents reportedly asked for no ➲

special privileges and treatment to be provided to the young prince during these sessions.

From 1958 to 1962, he moved to Cheam preparatory school in Berkshire, where his father had been a pupil and at that time was exclusively for boys. For his secondary education, the young prince was dispatched to Gordonstoun School near Elgin in northeastern Scotland. Again, the Duke of Edinburgh had been a pupil and he was determined that his son would experience its unique features.

The school was founded in 1934 as the British Salem School by German-Jewish educator Kurt Hahn and unlike traditional public schools of that period put great emphasis on team work, leadership and overcoming adversity. The main vehicle for creating this was a Spartan regime of cold showers, no-nonsense food and lots of strenuous outdoor activities in the nearby Highlands or Moray Firth.

When Prince Charles was quoted as describing Gordonstoun, as "Colditz in kilts" - in a

Queen Elizabeth II was a keen amateur photographer and recorded key events of Charles' early life. (Corbis Hulton Deutsch Getty)

reference to the infamous World War Two German prisoner of war camp - it was apparent that he was less than happy during his time at the school. Although he subsequently praised Gordonstoun, stating it had taught him "a great deal about myself and my own abilities and disabilities. It taught me to accept challenges and take the initiative," he said. In another in interview, he said he was "glad" he had attended Gordonstoun and that the "toughness of the place" was "much exaggerated". Although, it should be noted that he did not send his two sons to the school.

As he was coming to end of his time at Gordonstoun in 1966, the now adolescent prince was dispatched to Australia to spend two terms at the Timbertop campus of Geelong Grammar School in Victoria. During his time 'Down Under' he visited Papua New Guinea on a school trip with his history tutor, Michael Collins Persse.

In another royal first, Prince Charles finished

In the 1960s the royal family opened themselves up for public scrutiny in a ground breaking television documentary. (Hulton Archive Getty)

Charles helps his younger brother, Edward, control a go-cart in the grounds of a royal palace. (Hulton Archive Getty)

Charles' grandparents, King George VI, and Queen Elizabeth, were ever present during his early years. Here he has just been christened. (Nederlands Fotocollectie Anefo)

In the 1960s millions of television viewers saw a human side of the royal family relaxing on the Balmoral Estate. (Hulton Archive Getty)

"There is an urban myth that the prince's bodyguard – who had to accompany him to all his lectures – sat the same exams and got a better result."

his education in 1967 with six GCE O-levels and two A-levels in history and French, at grades B and C respectively.

Then, rather than go straight into the armed forces, Prince Charles again broke with royal tradition and, in October 1967, was enrolled as an undergraduate student at Trinity College at Cambridge University. He began studying archaeology and anthropology but then changed to history for the second part of his studies. There has been some debate about whether the prince's exam results were good enough on their own to earn him a place at one of Britain's most prestigious universities. However, there was never any chance of his application being rejected. After all, his distant relative, Henry VIII, had founded Trinity College in 1546.

Photographs of Cambridge's most high profile student show him walking the streets of the city in his gown and tie, which seems incongruously at odds with the image of the 1960s as the era of student radicalism, flower power and hippies.

University life allowed Prince Charles to indulge his love of British comedy and he joined the legendary Cambridge University Footlights dramatic club, which over the years has launched the careers of dozens of comedians, including Peter Cook, John Bird, half of Monty Python, Stephen Fry, Sacha Baron Cohen, and Armstrong & Miller. The prince famously took

Charles attended Gordonstoun public school in northeast Scotland between 1962 and 1966, which was famous for its robust outdoor-based curriculum and activities. (Laura Oak)

part in a number of shows – which received mixed reviews – and on one occasion appeared wearing a rubbish bin.

Later, he would fondly recall his time at Cambridge and the lively nights spent in Trinity College, saying, "he had to accustom [himself] to, particularly the grinding note of an [Cambridge] Urban District Council dust lorry's engine rising and falling in spasmodic bursts of agonised energy at 7 o'clock in the morning, accompanied by the monotonous, jovial dustman's refrain of 'O come, All Ye Faithful' and the head-splitting clang of the dustbins."

"At night too, it was also hard to ignore the timeless notes of the *National Anthem* or *'Land of My Fathers'*, punctuated by the melodious disintegration of bottles and merry voices raised in conversation, reaching the barred confines of [his] room at some unearthly dark watches of the night."

It is not clear how much time Prince Charles actually devoted to his studies while at university. He found time to learn to fly with the university air squadron, he was invested as Prince of Wales and for a term, during his second year, he attended the University College of Wales in Aberystwyth, studying Welsh history and language.

There is a popular urban myth that the prince's bodyguard – who had to accompany him to all his lectures – sat the same exams and got a better result. It was never proved.

In June 1970, Prince Charles graduated with a 2:2 Bachelor of Arts degree, making him the first British heir apparent to earn a university degree. ●

Prince Charles in 1972 in a classic pose for the high society photographer Allan Warren. (Allan Warren)

A NEW PRINCE FOR A NEW ERA

The Investiture of the Prince of Wales

A statue of Owain Glyndŵr in Corwen town square. As the last Welsh-born Prince of Wales he is a symbol to Welsh nationalists, who complain the historic title has been usurped by the British royal family. (Michael Garlick)

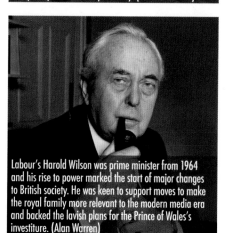

Labour's Harold Wilson was prime minister from 1964 and his rise to power marked the start of major changes to British society. He was keen to support moves to make the royal family more relevant to the modern media era and backed the lavish plans for the Prince of Wales's investiture. (Alan Warren)

There were protests by Welsh nationalists against the investiture of Prince Charles at Caernarfon Castle in North Wales. (Geoff Charles)

In a made for television moment at Caernarfon Castle in July 1969, Prince Charles was publicly acknowledged as Prince of Wales. The ancient title for the heir apparent to the British monarchy originated in 1301 when the English King Edward I, after completing his conquest of Wales, gave the title to his heir, Prince Edward, later Edward II.

In a bid to placate the newly subjugated population, Edward reputedly offered his baby son who was born in Caernarfon to the Welsh as a prince "that was borne in Wales and could speak never a word of English." The story has entered the folklore around the Prince of Wales title but there is little historical evidence to support the claims.

In the 18th and 19th centuries the epithet fell out of fashion with the British royal family, and it became a largely symbolic title that was conveyed in letters or investitures in the House of Lords in London.

The Welsh-born Prime Minister David Lloyd George was instrumental in the revival of the tradition of investing the Prince of Wales in the principality in a bid to head off a growth in Welsh nationalism. King George V invested his son, the future King Edward VIII, in a ceremony at Caernarfon Castle in 1911. There had never been a Princess of Wales, so Elizabeth did not adopt the title when her father took the throne in 1936.

During the 1960s, Queen Elizabeth II was keen to revive the tradition of the investiture as a bid to reinforce the royal family's links to Wales. The then government of Harold Wilson was keen to support the move. Charles had already received the title Prince of Wales in 1958 by the issuing

of letters patent but by 1969 it was decided a public investiture would be held at Caernarfon Castle. Princess Margaret's husband, the society photographer Antony Armstrong-Jones, designed the distinctive investiture set with its memorable canopy.

To prepare Charles to make part of the investiture address in Welsh, he was dispatched for nine months to Aberystwyth University to learn the language and absorb himself in Welsh culture. Important parts of the investiture were to be conducted in Welsh, so it was vital that Charles sounded convincing when speaking the native tongue of the principality.

The investiture ceremony on July 1, 1969 took place in superb weather. The 20-year-old prince approached Queen Elizabeth II and the Duke of Edinburgh sitting under the canopy in the castle's courtyard.

As he came to the stage Charles knelt before the three thrones on the stage. During the

Caernarfon Castle was transformed for the investiture ceremony with a set designed by The Queen's brother-in-law and high society photographer, Antony Armstrong Jones. (Dr Charles Nelson/Caernarfon Castle)

> "Welsh public support the monarchy and wish for Prince William to assume the title when his father becomes monarch"

reading of the letters of patent in Welsh, his mother invested Prince Charles with the girdle, sword, coronet, ring, rod and kingly mantle, in that order. Prince Charles then declared, "I, Charles, Prince of Wales, do become your liege man of life and limb and of earthly worship, and faith and truth I will bear unto thee, to live and die against all manner of folks."

Charles then customarily kissed his mother's cheek and they embraced. Charles then took his place in the throne at his mother's right, before standing to give two speeches, one in Welsh and one in English.

Despite protests both in the run up to the event and on the day of the ceremony by Welsh Nationalists, the investiture was a public relations triumph. The showpiece was broadcast live on television and the audiences dwarfed the number of protestors, 19 million Britons tuned in to watch the event and it attracted more than 500m viewers worldwide. Opinion polls since 1969 have consistently reported a large majority of the Welsh public support the monarchy and wish for Prince William to assume the title when his father becomes monarch.

The political sensitivities around the investiture were revealed when government papers were released under the 30 year rule. The Labour Secretary of State for Wales wrote to the Prime Minister after the investiture, protesting about the Prince's speech. George Thomas complained that the Prince had talked about "cultural and political awakening in Wales" and that such a statement was "most helpful for the Nationalists." ●

THE KING'S MILITARY LINKS

Life in Uniform

In his youth The King was a qualified military helicopter pilot. (@RoyalFamily)

British monarchs have long been associated with the country's armed forces. This dates back to the days when monarchs would lead their troops into battle, sharing the risks and dangers with their men as they battled both foreign and domestic foes.

The last British monarch to head an army into action was George II, who stood with his red coated troops at the Battle of Dettingen on June 27, 1743. It was one of the first battlefield successes of the newly professional British Army, which defeated stronger Austrian troops thanks to better fire discipline. The commanding officer of The Royal Scots Fusiliers, Lieutenant Colonel Sir Andrew Agnew of Lochnaw, famously ordered his regiment not to fire until "they could see the whites of the enemy's eyes."

George II's role in this victory was minimal and his professional officers requested that in future The King leave the business of war to them. Colonel Agnew was quoted as telling The King. "Ay, please Your Majesty, but they didna' gang back again."

Since then, British monarchs, have as a rule followed his advice and stepped back from being active warrior Kings or Queens. Although formally the commander-in-chief of British armed forces, modern British monarchs have not taken an executive role in their affairs. The monarch and other members of the royal family perform ceremonial functions and have honour roles, but government ministers are responsible for the political control and operational direction of the armed forces. This is a unique British arrangement and is an extension of the guiding principles of the British constitutional monarchy. The King represents the country and armed forces but does not run them on a day-to-day basis, that job is passed to elected government ministers and the professional military commanders.

That does not mean the monarch and the royal family do not have influence and interest in the armed forces. According to Buckingham Palace, "The King is a strong supporter of the armed services and saw them as one of the most important parts of his role as heir to The Throne."

The Prince of Wales's relationship with the armed services consisted of three main activities:

● Promoting the role of the armed services within national life, through operational visits, ceremonial duties, and commemorative activity across the UK and around the world.
● Supporting the welfare and interests of service personnel, veterans, and their families.
● Maintaining the history and heritage of the armed services through links with regiments, units and formations both in the UK and around the Commonwealth.

While this involved many days attending parades and other functions, it also involve hard work keeping on top of issues, keeping in touch with key individuals and bringing key players together to shape agendas.

As Prince of Wales, and now monarch, ➲

King Charles III has spent much of his life serving in uniform and maintaining his links with the armed forces of Britain and the Commonwealth.

His first exposure to military life came during his second year at Cambridge University where he learned to fly the Chipmunk aircraft with Cambridge University Air Squadron. In March 1971, the Prince flew himself to Royal Air Force College Cranwell in Lincolnshire, to begin training as an RAF officer.

Six months later, after the passing out at Cranwell as a flight lieutenant, he embarked on a naval career, following in the footsteps of his father, grandfather and both his great-grandfathers. A six-week course at the Royal Naval College, Dartmouth, was followed first by service on the guided missile destroyer HMS *Norfolk* and two frigates. The Prince then qualified as a Wessex helicopter pilot in 1974 before joining 845 Naval Air Squadron, which operated from the commando carrier HMS Hermes. On February 9, 1976, The Prince took command of the small coastal mine hunter, HMS *Bronington*, for his last nine months in the Navy.

Despite ending his fulltime naval service, he continued to build his affiliations with all branches of the British and Commonwealth armed forces.

His first honorary appointment in the armed forces was as colonel in chief of the Royal Regiment of Wales in 1969. Since then, he has also been installed as colonel in chief, colonel, honorary air commodore, air commodore in chief, deputy colonel in chief, royal honorary colonel, royal colonel, and honorary commodore of at least 32 military formations throughout the Commonwealth.

The young prince was determined not just to been seen as a remote figurehead of the military units he had an affiliation with and on several occasions joined in with their training. For example, after his appointment as colonel in chief of The Parachute Regiment in 1977 he requested to join a Parachute Training Course at RAF Brize Norton to qualify for his parachute jump wings. Parachuting was not new to ➲

Taking part in rigorous military training was part of the then Prince of Wales' royal duties, including joining Royal Marines recruits on a commando assault course. @RoyalFamily)

In July 2022 the then Prince of Wales visited HMS Queen Elizabeth to meet veterans of the 1982 Falklands conflict and pay tribute to service personnel who made the ultimate sacrifice in that war. (MOD/Crown Copyright)

In November 2022 King Charles III led the nation at the Cenotaph in London to pay tribute to Britain and the Commonwealth's war dead. (MOD/Crown Copyright)

The monarch has a special relationship with the regiments of the Household Division who participate in ceremonial events on major royal occasions. (MOD/Crown Copyright)

In October 2022, The King assumed the position of captain general of the Royal Marines on the 358th anniversary of the elite unit being formed by his ancestor King Charles II in 1664. (@RoyalFamily)

The King and other member of the royal family use the aircraft of 32 (The Royal) Squadron on official duties. Since 2022 the squadron has been re-equipped with two Dassault Envoy executive jets, which replaced the previous BAe 146 aircraft. (MOD/Crown Copyright)

the Prince of Wales who had made his first parachute drop when he was aged 23 in July 1971 from an Andover aircraft into Studland Bay, Dorset.

The Prince of Wales continued his association with the famous 'Red Devils' in the following years, including regularly travelling to Normandy and Arnhem to honour the sacrifice of Paras during commemorative events for those who fell in those iconic World War Two battles. In July 2021, he presented the new colours to The Parachute Regiment at their Merville Barracks base in Colchester. Addressing soldiers, veterans, and families he told the parade: "I find it hard to believe that it's been 44 years since I became your colonel in chief and nearly 50 years since I made my first parachute drop, initially upside down with my legs in the rigging lines, into Studland Bay, Dorset, where I was pulled out of the water by the Royal Marines."

Unlike his brother Andrew and son Harry, as heir to the throne the then Prince of Wales was not allowed to go on active operations during his time in uniform. This decision was made by his mother and government ministers on security grounds. He did, however, visit British forces in Iraq and Afghanistan and was allowed to travel to frontline positions in downtown Basra in 2004 and Helmand province in 2010.

In a rare pool interview with journalists during his visit, the then Prince of Wales said he had tried four times to get to Afghanistan before finally being allowed to make his trip in March 2010.

Over time the insignia on the colours and standards of British Army regiments, RAF squadrons, and Royal Navy ships will be changed to incorporate the new monarch's regalia. (MOD/Crown Copyright)

"I have quite a large number of regiments of which I am colonel in chief ... so, while my people are out here, I wanted to come and see them and, sadly, it has been difficult up until this time," he said. "I am thrilled to have got here at last because I just wanted to see the kind of conditions they were in and also to try to generally take an interest and encourage."

He described the Rifles regiment, which had lost a number of troops in the previous few weeks – notably in the Sangin area – as having "a bloody awful time". He added: "My heart goes out to them and their families."

The visit took place two years after Prince Harry had served in Afghanistan, he said. "As a parent, you worry the whole time. I think, if you are out here, you are getting on with everything and it's not the same. But, for everyone left behind, it's ghastly. But having said that, ... The families are the most wonderful support to their

The then Prince of Wales meets Royal Air Force officers during a visit to the RAF College at Cranwell. (MOD/Crown Copyright)

The King enjoys talking to service personnel of all ranks and ages. (MOD/Crown Copyright)

"I find it hard to believe that it's been 44 years since I became your colonel in chief and nearly 50 years since I made my first parachute drop"

loved ones."

Since 2009, the future King held the second-highest ranks in all three branches of the Canadian forces and, in June 2012, the Queen awarded him the highest honorary rank in all three services of the British armed forces, "to acknowledge his support in her role as commander in chief," installing him as admiral of the fleet, field marshal and marshal of the Royal Air Force.

During the following decade, the future King took on many of the ceremonial duties from his mother. The most prominent sign of this was when he laid the first Remembrance Day wreath at the Cenotaph on behalf his mother in November 2017.

After his ascent to the throne in September 2022, The King immediately became the commander in chief or head of the British and many Commonwealth armed forces. Some things changed immediately. Officers now hold

The King's Commission and all new recruits started to swear allegiance to The King.

Other changes are being introduced over time to avoid wasting money and causing unnecessary disruption. At the new King's insistence the new royal cipher will not immediately be changed on regimental colours and rank badges.

The King's affiliations to military units is also in a period of transition. He has not immediately taken over all the honorary affiliations held by his mother, except in the case of regiments of the Household Division, where the monarch is automatically their colonel in chief. In October 2022, Buckingham Palace announced that The King would assume the role of captain general of the Royal Marines. This ceremonial role as head of the elite corps had been vacant since February 2021 when Prince Harry had stood down. The King's father had held the post for 64 years.

In the case of the late Queen's other military affiliations no decisions have been made whether The King or other members of the royal family will take them over. As part of this review The King's remaining affiliations are expected to also be reviewed and possibly redistributed. Similar exercises are being undertaken in Commonwealth countries.

The King's affiliations with the regiments of the Household Division will be on full display on June 17 this year when he participates in his first Trooping of the Colour parade as monarch. More than 1,400 parading Guardsmen, 200 horses and 400 military musicians will come together to put on a display of military precision, horsemanship and fanfare to mark The King's official birthday. ●

THE
DIANA

The First Royal Marriage

Britain in 1981 was a very different country. Unemployment had hit 2.5m and was rising. Riots had ravaged Brixton, Moss Side and Toxteth. Prime Minister Margaret Thatcher had just declared that she was "not for turning" and the opposition Labour Party was engulfed by in-fighting. This was only the start of a decade of political confrontation, economic upheaval, and social strife.

So, when the engagement of the Prince of Wales and Lady Diana Spencer was announced on February 24, 1981, it was a rare item of welcome good news. Over the next five months news of the preparation for the wedding of the decade was an entertaining distraction from other gloomy headlines.

St Paul's Cathedral was the venue for the marriage of royal couple on July 29, 1981. It is hard to imagine a more fairy-tale event which was watched by a global television audience of more than 750m and more than a billion listened to the service on the radio. This was more than for the 1969 moon landing.

Everything about the royal wedding was done on a lavish scale. Just over 3,500 guests made up the congregation in the cathedral. Three choirs

> ## "It is hard to imagine a more fairy-tale event which was watched by a global television audience of more than 750m and more than a billion listened to the service on the radio. "

and orchestras performed. The royal family were carried in eight carriages. More than 2,000 military personnel were on duty and 4,000 police officers guarded the event. According to some estimates the price tag eventually ran to £57m.

The venue was switched from the traditional site of royal weddings, Westminster Abbey to St Paul's to allow a bigger congregation and a longer procession through London. Two million members of the public turned out to get a sight of the happy couple.

The Church of England ceremony was presided over by Robert Runcie, Archbishop of Canterbury, and the Very Reverend Alan Webster, Dean of St Paul's Cathedral.

Diana arrived in the State Glass Coach, accompanied by her father Earl Spencer, and immediately wowed the global audience when she emerged wearing her ivory silk taffeta wedding dress, decorated with lace, hand embroidery, sequins, and 10,000 pearls. The dress, designed by Elizabeth and David Emanuel, cost £9,000 and had a 7.6m long train of ivory taffeta and antique lace, which was reputed to ➲

YEARS

The royal couple were welcomed around the world as politicians, statesmen, rock stars and other celebrities tried to benefit from the 'Diana Effect'. Here they visit US President Ronald Reagan in the White House. (White House)

be longest train in the history of royal weddings. Five bridesmaids and two page boys assisted in the bride's progress into the cathedral.

Inside the cathedral were members of European royal families, government leaders and Commonwealth governor generals, military chiefs and US First Lady, Nancy Reagan. The bride invited the staff of the nursery school in which she had worked prior to the wedding. Charles' favourite comedians, Spike Milligan and Harry Secombe were also watching on.

Charles wore his full dress naval commander's uniform, with assorted decorations, gold epaulettes and a dress sword. He was accompanied by his brothers, Andrew and Edward, who were dubbed his supporters, the equivalent of 'best men' for royal weddings.

As per tradition, the bride walked up the aisle to join her husband at the altar. The two were nervous. Diana accidentally changed the order of Charles's names during her vows, saying "Philip Charles Arthur George" instead of the correct "Charles Philip Arthur George". She did not promise to "obey" him as part of the traditional vows. That word was eliminated at the couple's request, which caused a sensation

at the time. Charles also made an error. He said he would offer her "thy goods" instead of "my worldly goods".

After the ceremony, the couple returned to Buckingham Palace in an open top carriage through cheering crowds and then made the traditional appearance on the palace balcony. At 1.10pm he famously kissed his bride to roars of approval from the huge gathering outside the palace and along the Mall.

The couple and 120 guests attended the wedding breakfast in the palace, which featured

> "HIV does not make people dangerous to know. You can shake their hands and give them a hug. Heaven knows they need it."

27 wedding cakes. The main cake was a five-foot-tall, layered fruitcake which weighed 225 pounds.

After the festivities, the couple left the palace in a State Landau, bearing a 'Just Married' sign and headed over Westminster Bridge to catch the Royal Train from Waterloo to Romsey in Hampshire to spend the wedding night at Lord Louis Mountbatten's Broadlands estate. They then flew to Gibraltar to join the Royal Yacht Britannia for a Mediterranean honeymoon cruise.

Celebrity

The first royal wedding of the 1980s transformed the royal family into a global celebrity brand. Charles and Diana, now titled the Princess of Wales, subsequently toured the world, wowing audience on every continent. These visits generated iconic images of the royal couple that still resonate today. Whether it be Princess Diana dancing with John Travolta in the White House or sitting alone outside the Taj Mahal in New Delhi. Not surprisingly, for a period in time Princess Diana became the most photographed woman in the world.

Hollywood royalty, John Travolta, dances with British royalty, Princess Diana, in the White House. (White House)

Australians could not get enough of dazzling princess. (Queensland State Archive)

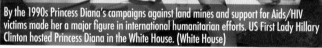
By the 1990s Princess Diana's campaigns against land mines and support for Aids/HIV victims made her a major figure in international humanitarian efforts. US First Lady Hillary Clinton hosted Princess Diana in the White House. (White House)

Princess Diana's visits were always memorable. (Newcastle Libraries)

Princess Diana criss-crossed Britain and the world visiting a wide range of organisations and groups, establishing her reputation as someone who could communicate and empathise with ordinary people. Here she visits the West Midlands Police. (West Midlands Police)

Over the next decade a roller coaster of events unfolded as the global fame of the royal family collided with their real lives.

Prince William was born in June 1982 and Prince Harry arrived in September 1984. Their mother took a close interest in their upbringing and many royal traditions were broken. They attended primary school near to Kensington Palace and their mother did the school run.

Despite their involvement in high profile royal events and state ceremonial occasions, it was becoming increasingly obvious to observers that the royal couple had very different interests. He consulted with alternative medicine gurus and went to the opera. She took her children to theme parks and enjoyed Duran Duran concerts.

At the height of the concern about the spread of HIV/AIDS in the late 1980s, Prince Diana went out of her way to try to dispel public suspicion of victims and, in 1987 was photographed holding hands with an AIDS patient. She said at the time, "HIV does not make people dangerous to know. You can shake their hands and give them a hug. Heaven knows they need it. What's more, you can share their homes, their workplaces, and their playgrounds and toys."

It became apparent that the royal couple's marriage was in trouble and soon it was being

Across the Commonwealth the 1981 royal wedding was celebrated in some style. (New Zealand Archives)

widely reported in the media. Both the Prince of Wales and Princess Diana started to appear in the media to give their sides of the story. The Prince gave an television interview to broadcaster Jonathan Dimbleby. Princess Diana provided material for Andrew Morton's book, Diana: Her True Story. Then recordings of intimate telephone conversations between the Prince and Mrs Camilla Parker-Bowles and Prince Diana and James Gilbey appeared in the media.

The first round of 'War of the Wales' culminated in December 1992, with the Prime Minister John Major announcing the couple's "amicable separation" to the House of Commons. This truce did not last long and very

soon the newspapers were full of more stories about the royal couple's problems. Princess Diana's global profile grew exponentially. After she joined the international campaign to ban anti-personnel land mines, Princess Diana became one the world's most high profile humanitarian advocates. Presidents, prime ministers, and other world leaders were falling over themselves to be photographed with her. For the Prince of Wales, this was two pronged problem. His wife's campaigning struck a chord with the zeitgeist of the time and his interests appeared a bit fringe. This also made it almost impossible for the prince's advocates to make his case in media, without appearing begrudging and mean. This was one media battle the heir to

Everywhere Prince Diana went huge crowds of well wishers appeared. (Russ Quinlan)

Diana's enduring legacy. In July 2021 on what would have been her 60th Birthday large tributes were left outside her former home at Kensington Palace. (Sahaib3005)

Princess Diana's death in 1997 saw a national outpouring of grief. (Maxwell Hamilton)

short her holiday to return to London and made an unprecedented live televised tribute to the Princess Diana.

Diana's funeral took place in Westminster Abbey on September 6 and produced even more dramatic scenes. Princes William and Harry walked in the funeral procession behind her coffin, along with her ex-husband, the Duke of Edinburgh, and her brother Lord Spencer.

In his oration, Lord Spencer said of his sister: "She proved in the last year that she needed no royal title to continue to generate her particular brand of magic." Elton John performed a specially adapted version of his song, Candle in the Wind, with the opening line amended to "Goodbye England's rose, may you ever grow in our hearts".

The funeral was televised live and 31m people in Britain watched, with a global audience estimated at more than two billion.

For the Prince of Wales and his family, the death of Princess Diana was a watershed moment. For tragic reasons, the 'War of the Wales' was brought to an abrupt end.

The tragic events on August 31, 1977 and the week that followed appeared to make everyone – royal family members and their friends, journalists, and commentators - take a step back and wonder if events had just gotten out of hand.

There was almost universal sympathy for her two sons and the British media agreed a 'truce' with Buckingham Palace to limit coverage of the young princes while they were at school and university.

It was not quite a 'year zero' moment, but it was clear that nothing would be the same again for Britain's royal family. ●

> "Elton John performed a specially adapted version of his song, Candle in the Wind, with the opening line amended to "Goodbye England's rose, may you ever grow in our hearts."

the throne just could not win.

After Princess Diana gave an interview to the BBC, which was broadcast in November 1995, Buckingham Palace announced that the royal couple would divorce. The interview included the now famous comment from the Princess: "Well, there were three of us in this marriage, so it was a bit crowded."

The divorce of the heir apparent, which was finalised on August 28, 1996, was unprecedented and was a sign that the royal family had moved on dramatically from the days of the abdication of Edward VIII in 1936.

If that was not dramatic enough a year later, Princess Diana would die in horrific circumstances in Paris. In the early hours of August 31, 1997, the Princess was travelling with her companion, Dodi Fayed, from the Ritz

Hotel when their car crashed in the Pont de l'Alma tunnel. The Princess died later in hospital, setting off an unprecedented week of mourning.

The events of the following week rocked the royal family. Prime Minister Tony Blair called Diana, 'The People's Princess'. Crowds gathered outside royal residences in London to lay tributes and show their respects. Newspapers criticised Queen Elizabeth II for staying at Balmoral in Scotland and complained that the flags were not flying at half mast on Buckingham Palace. Queen Elizabeth II cut

The funeral of Princess Diana was one of the most iconic events of the 1990s. (Paddy Briggs)

Government ministers famously dreaded receiving a so-called 'black spider memo' from the then Prince of Wales. These missives were often enlivened with handwritten exclamation marks and comments in black ink from the heir to the throne, hence the nickname.

When the existence of the letters became public, a concerted campaign was launched under the Freedom of Information Act to get them published. After they were released, it became clear that the heir to the throne had

strong opinions about many things and was not afraid to use his standing and publicity to let a posse of hapless ministers and officials know when he thought they were doing something silly or that he disagreed with.

In 2006, Mark Bolland, the Prince's former deputy private secretary revealed that the Prince had referred to himself as a 'dissident' who worked against the prevailing political consensus. This resulted in the Prince of Wales "routinely meddling in political issues… and wrote sometimes in extreme terms to ministers, members of parliament and others

in positions of political power and influence," said Bollard. "The prince used all the means of communication at his disposal, including meetings with ministers and others, speeches, and correspondence with leaders in all walks of life and politicians. He was never party-political, but to argue that he was not political was difficult."

On his accession to the throne last year, King Charles III has been re-assessing his involvement in many of his charities and other organisations. "My life will of course change as I take up my new responsibilities," the new King said in his

SETTING THE AGENDA

The King's Interests

In touch with the natural world. The Prince of Wales inaugurating the Wiltshire Wildlife Trust's reserve at Clattinger Farm, Near Oaksey, Wiltshire in 2009. (Tim Graham Photo Library/ Getty Images)

> "It will no longer be possible for me to give so much of my time and energies to the charities and issues for which I care so deeply."

first royal broadcast on September 9, 2022. "It will no longer be possible for me to give so much of my time and energies to the charities and issues for which I care so deeply. But I know this important work will go on in the trusted hands of others."

During the 1980s and 1990s, the then Prince of Wales developed strong interests in the natural world, environment issues and architecture. He put many of his ideas into practice on his Duchy of Cornwall estate, including establishing the Duchy Originals brand of organically farmed products. For many years his views were sometimes dismissed as 'fringe', 'alternative' or 'weird hippy stuff' by some politicians or newspapers. However, in many areas his views – such as those on climate change - are now accepted as mainstream and suggest the future King was ahead of his time.

The shortcomings of modern building design were a particular interest and at gala dinner for architects in 1984 he famously criticised the extension to the National Gallery in London, calling it a "monstrous carbuncle on the face of a much-loved friend" and deplored the "glass stumps and concrete towers" of modern architecture. He asserted that "it is possible, and important in human terms, to respect old buildings, street plans and traditional scales and at the same time not to feel guilty about a preference for facades, ornaments, and soft materials," and called for local community involvement in architectural choices, asking, "Why can't we have those curves and arches that express feeling in design? What is wrong with them? Why has everything got to be vertical, straight, unbending, only at right angles – and functional?"

The comments generated considerable controversy at the time amid accusations that the Prince of Wales was stuck in the past.

The development of the sustainable Poundbury village on Duchy of Cornwall land is the most recent example of the then Duke of Cornwall's commitment to improving the lived environment. The new Duke of Cornwall, Prince William has since taken over the direction and day-to-day management of the Duchy's estates.

King Charles III has long had an interest in countering climate change – even before it was fashionable – and made a speech at the opening ceremony for the COP26 climate conference in Glasgow in 2021 saying: "A vast, 'military-style campaign' was needed to marshal the strength of the global private sector, for tackling climate change."

On his own land, he installed biomass boilers and hydroelectric turbines in the rivers, as well as utilising solar panels at Clarence House and Highgrove House, using electric cars on his estates and running his Aston Martin DB6 on E85 ethanol fuel.

As Prince of Wales, he also had a keen interest in religion and spiritual issues, visiting non-Christian places of worship and meeting other faith leaders. He developed a strong friendship with the spiritual guru, Sir Laurens van der Post and is on close terms with many Islamic leaders and rulers around the Middle East.

As a young man, the Prince was a keen polo player but he suffered two injuries that prevented him from playing for as long as he would have liked. He regularly rode to hounds until fox hunting was banned in 2005 and is a noted salmon angler. And away from the field he's an avid painter in watercolours.

Perhaps his most high profile philanthropic activity was the setting up of the Prince's Trust in 1976 with the £7,500 he received as severance pay when he left the Royal Navy.

The idea was to improve the lives of disadvantaged young people

The Duchy of Cornwall Estate is now a leader in the growing and marketing of organic produce (Elina Mark)

The Duchy Original brand was the then Duke of Cornwall's contribution to bringing organic produce to the British shopper. (Lee Keoma)

by helping them secure career opportunities or simply to get their lives back on track. It supports eleven to 30-year-olds who are unemployed, struggling at school and at risk of exclusion. Many of the young people helped by the trust face issues such as homelessness, mental health problems, or trouble with the law.

The Trust runs a range of activities, which include helping young people start a business, residential personal development courses, and work experience and work-related training courses. There is also one to one support for participants and small monetary grants given to young people to help them get some training, education, or a job, as well as clubs in schools and projects to link young people with role models to boost their confidence.

In September 2020 the trust announced that it had helped 1,000,000 young people since its inception. The trust has a presence in every one of the United Kingdom's nations and spends

The King is keen to engage with wide audiences to win over support to his causes. (@RoyalFamily)

Organic agriculture has long been a passion of The King. (All Nite Images)

Wind turbines and their use in countering climate change is high up The King's agenda. (Rob Faulkner)

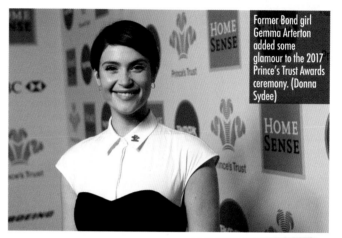

Former Bond girl Gemma Arterton added some glamour to the 2017 Prince's Trust Awards ceremony. (Donna Sydee)

just under £40m a year. It has over 1,100 staff and around 9,000 volunteers or secondees. In 2022 it supported over 46,000 young people across the UK, with three in four moving on to employment, education, volunteering, or training.

The Prince's Trust boasts some very famous alumni, who since achieving success of their own, support its fund raising efforts as ambassadors. Actor Idris Elba received a £1,500 grant that helped his start his career that took him to Hollywood. Selma star David Oyelowo and MOBO-winning music producer Naughty Boy were also among the Trust's prominent beneficiaries, along with the rock bands Elbow and The Stereophonics, who were helped up the music industry ladder by its support.

The King continues to take a close interest in the Trust he created and in a symbolic move, remained its president after becoming monarch. This signified the importance he placed on the Trust's work.

One real passion that he's nurtured from childhood is the mad cap radio series The Goon Show and he subsequently became honorary president of the Goon Show Preservation Society. Prince Charles became a lifelong friend of the leading Goon, Spike Milligan, and both made jokes at each other's expense.

When Milligan received a Lifetime Achievement Award at the British Comedy Awards in 1994, the Prince sent a congratulatory message to be read out on live television. The comedian interrupted the message to call the Prince a "little grovelling bastard" and later faxed the Prince, saying: "I suppose a knighthood is out of the question?" Seven years later, in 2001 the Prince arranged for the Irish comedian to receive an honorary knighthood. ●

The King is keen to engage with British industry as it seeks to win global market share. (BCB)

THE KING'S

Palaces, Country Houses and Estates

As head of the royal family, on his accession to the throne King Charles III took over the stewardship of Britain's historic royal residences.

The iconic Buckingham Palace and Windsor Castle are perhaps the most well-known of them and they - along with the Palace of Holyroodhouse in Edinburgh - are owned by the Crown on behalf of the nation.

These are The King's official residences, and they are the location of major ceremonial events or state functions involving the royal family.

These often culminated with the late Queen and other senior royals appearing on the balcony of Buckingham Palace to wave at cheering crowds. King Charles III is expected to make his first balcony appearance as monarch during the celebration of his coronation in May.

Buckingham Palace has served as the official London residence of British monarchs since 1837 and today is the administrative headquarters of the royal 'Firm'. It has 775 rooms, including 19 State rooms, 52 Royal and guest bedrooms, 188 staff bedrooms, 92 offices and 78 bathrooms. In measurements, the ➲

Buckingham Palace is the iconic London residence of The King and headquarters of the royal 'Firm'. (MOD)

HOMES

building is 108 metres long across the front, 120 metres deep (including the central quadrangle) and 24 metres high. The iconic front aspect of Buckingham Palace makes it a global landmark and a must-visit location for tourists from all over the world. In the summer months the palace is open to visitors, who call also to view the royal art collection and see the royal carriages in the palace Mews.

The palace is currently undergoing a major refurbishment, so The King has not yet taken up permanent residence. Until this work is complete The King and Queen Consort will continue to use nearby Clarence House as their London home.

Clarence House is one of several other royal residences in London, alongside Kensington Palace and St James's Palace. Other members of the extended family live in them.

Windsor Castle, in the Royal County of Berkshire, is the oldest and largest occupied castle in the world. It is open to visitors throughout the year. Founded by William the Conqueror in the 11th century, it has since been the home of 40 British monarchs. Queen Elizabeth II spent most of her private weekends at the Castle.

The Palace of Holyroodhouse stands at the end of Edinburgh's Royal Mile and has close associations with some of Scotland's most well-known historic figures such as Mary, Queen of Scots, and Bonnie Prince Charlie. Today it is used by The King when carrying out official engagements in Scotland.

The King also privately owns four other residences, including the famous Balmoral Castle and Estate, where Queen Elizabeth II passed away. Sandringham House and Estate in Norfolk was another of the late Queen's favourite residences. Nearby Balmoral is Birkhall Estate, which the then Prince of Wales inherited from his grandmother, Queen Elizabeth, The

Birkhall Estate on Royal Deeside was inherited by The King from his grandmother in 2002. (Alan Finlay)

Clarence House is King Charles III's London residence and he is set to stay there until 2027 while Buckingham Palace undergoes renovations. (ChrisO)

Queen Mother in 2002.

The private property most associated with The King is Highgrove House and Estate in Gloucestershire, which was purchased by the Duchy of Cornwall for his use in 1980. Over the decades he made the house his own, resetting the gardens and turning the farms on the estate over to organic farming techniques. As the property is owned by the Duchy of Cornwall, it passed to the new Prince of Wales, William, after Queen Elizabeth II's death in September, 2022.

Over the centuries British monarchs built several palaces and residences that are no longer in day-to-day use by today's royal family. Among them are some of the most historic and iconic buildings in Britain and these are maintained by the Historic Royal Palaces charity that operates independently from the royal family. These include the Tower of London, which is home to the Crown Jewels; Hampton Court Palace; The Banqueting House in Whitehall; Kew Palace in Richmond, West London, and Hillsborough Castle in Northern Ireland. These are all open for the public to visit.

In addition to his royal and private residences, The King holds two large property portfolios

The Palace of Holyroodhouse in Edinburgh is The King's official residence when he visits the Scottish capital. (XtoF)

Windsor Castle in the Royal County of Berkshire was reputed to be The Queen's favourite residence. (Diliff)

Balmoral Estate in the Scottish Highlands on Royal Deeside has been a private residence of British monarchs since Queen Victoria's time. (Stuart Yates)

that generate income to fund the royal family. The surplus over and above these routine annual running costs are paid to the Treasury to fund government expenditure. The largest is the Crown Estates, which controls assets worth £15.6bn, including properties in central London, 7,920km2 of agricultural land and forest and more than half of the UK's foreshore. In 2022 the Crown Estates generated £490m in revenue.

The monarch, as the Duke of Lancaster, controls the Duchy of Lancaster, which consists of 45,550 acres of land holdings, including rural estates and farmland, urban developments, historic buildings and some commercial properties across England and Wales, particularly in Cheshire, Staffordshire, Derbyshire, Lincolnshire, Yorkshire,

Highgrove House in Gloucestershire has been The King's private residence since 1980. (Andrew Berry)

Lancashire, and the Savoy Estate in London. It generated a surplus more than £20m in 2017. The Duchy of Cornwall is controlled separately by the Prince of Wales and has land holdings in England of 135,000 acres. In 2017–18 it generated income of £21.7m.

Annually some 15% of the profits from these royal estates are usually made available to The King and the royal family to fund their official duties and maintain the royal residences, via a mechanism, known as the Sovereign Grant. This replaced the old Civil List funding mechanism in 2011. As well as day-to-day expenses, the Sovereign Grant is currently funding a major project to renovate Buckingham Palace and in 2017 the grant was raised from 15% to 25% of Crown Estates profits for a 10 year period. ●

Visiting the Royal Residences

One of the consequences of the November 1992 Windsor Castle fire was the opening of Buckingham Palace to visits by members of the public. The success of this venture led to a wider opening of royal residences. There are now a number of opportunities to look behind the scenes of The King's homes around Britain during 2023.

Buckingham Palace
It is possible to explore the magnificent State Rooms which are open to visitors for 10 weeks each summer (July 14 – September 4) and on selected dates during winter and spring.

The Royal Mews, Buckingham Palace
Open March 2 to October 30

The Queen's Gallery, Palace of Holyroodhouse
Temporarily closed

Windsor Castle
Open: Thursday - Monday

Frogmore House
Frogmore House and Gardens is open to pre-booked groups of 15 or more.

The Queen's Gallery, Buckingham Palace
Open Thursday - Monday

The Palace of Holyroodhouse in Edinburgh
Open: Thursday - Monday

To visit any of the royal residences visitors need to book in advance, via www.rct.uk/visit

Balmoral, Sandringham, High Grove, and Birkhall are privately owned by The King and are not routinely open to the public. However, occasionally special events are held in their grounds.

CAMILLA

Queen Consort

The Royal couple outside St Paul's Cathedral after the service of thanksgiving during the Platinum Jubilee for Queen Elizabeth in June 2022. (MOD/Crown Copyright)

By tradition, 'Queen Consort' is the unofficial title of the wife of a reigning British King, and she usually shares her spouse's social rank and status. George VI and all his predecessor's wives were officially titled 'Queen' but did not formally share The King's political and military powers, unless on occasion acting as regent. These Queens held the feminine equivalent of The King's monarchical titles and were crowned and anointed but were universally known as a consort to signify they held none of their husband's formal powers.

This was not the case with Queen Elizabeth II who was a queen regnant, who ruled suo jure (in her own right) and became Queen by inheriting the throne upon the death of her father, George VI. Her consort, Prince Philip, Duke of Edinburgh, was not crowned king because he was not the monarch and had no formal constitutional position in the execution of state business.

The wife of King Charles III was formally declared Queen Consort on the death of his mother, but it had been pre-announced in the late Queen's 2022 Accession Day message, published to mark the 70th anniversary of her

"It is intended that Mrs Parker Bowles should use the title HRH The Princess Consort when the Prince of Wales accedes to the throne."

reign. Queen Elizabeth II stated that it was her "sincere wish" for Camilla to be known as Queen Consort upon Charles's accession to the throne.

Her formal title is a new innovation, with the previous wives of British monarch's simply being called 'Queen' and this stems from the fact that for the first time Britain has a monarch who is divorced and re-married. The fallout from the then Prince of Wales' divorce and the popularity of his late wife, Princess Diana, meant the issue of Camilla Parker Bowles becoming 'Queen' had to handled with considerable sensitivity.

Before his second marriage in 2005, the Prince of Wales issued a statement saying: "Mrs Parker Bowles will use the title HRH The Duchess of Cornwall after marriage. It is intended that Mrs Parker Bowles should use the title HRH The Princess Consort when the Prince of Wales accedes to the throne."

However, in the intervening years, public opinion softened towards The King's new wife and as Queen Elizabeth II celebrated her Platinum Jubilee, she issued her statement about Camilla becoming the Queen Consort. She will be crowned alongside her husband at The King's coronation in May and the Queen Mary's crown has been removed from the display of royal jewels at the Tower of London to be reworked for the purpose. ➲

Camilla's mother was the daughter of the 3rd Baron Ashcombe. Her father was a decorated army officer in World War Two, who subsequently became a wine merchant to high society. Major Shand, MC and Bar, was Vice Lord-Lieutenant of East Sussex and Master of the South Downs Hounds for 19 years.

Born Camilla Rosemary Shand on July 17, 1947, she lived with her family in East Sussex from 1951. She left school before sitting A-Levels and subsequently headed to Switzerland to attend a finishing school and studied at the Institut Britannique in Paris. After returning to London in 1965, she became a debutante, although at this point the tradition of presenting eligible young ladies to the monarch at court had ended.

After working as a secretary and receptionist in London, Camilla married Guard's officer, Andrew Parker Bowles in July 1973. Guests at the wedding reception included Queen Elizabeth, Queen Mother, Princess Margaret, and Princess Anne. The couple had two children, Thomas Henry, and Laura Rose, born in 1974 and 1978 respectively. Brigadier Parker Bowles

The Duchess of Cornwall speaks to the crowds during the Commonwealth Heads of Government Meeting in 2018. (The Big Lunch)

> **"Princess Diana famously commented, "Well, there were three of us in this marriage, so it was a bit crowded."**

filed for divorce in 1994, and the marriage was dissolved in 1995.

The King and his wife have known each other since the early 1970s and shared many friends in social circles linked to polo, horse riding events and London clubs. The two were friends prior to Camilla's first marriage and there are reports that marriage was considered, with the Queen Mother reportedly approving. In the end, the King went off to join the Royal Navy and Camilla married Parker Bowles.

Throughout the marriage of the then Prince of Wales to Princess Diana there were reports that the couple had rekindled their relationship. Princess Diana famously commented, "Well, there were three of us in this marriage, so it was a bit crowded."

In the wake of Princess Diana's death in 1997, the Prince of Wales was free to marry Camilla, but there was a strong lobby in the media against the heir to the throne marrying her.

It took several years before the couple were able to marry. In 1999, they started attending functions together. A year later, Camilla met Queen Elizabeth II at a birthday party for the former King of Greece. Joint engagements

Queen Elizabeth II and the Duchess of Cornwall together in a royal carriage during the 2012 Golden Jubilee celebrations. (Ben London)

Boosting military morale was an important part of the Duchess of Cornwall's official duties. (MOD/Crown Copyright)

The Duchess of Cornwall was at her husband's side on many official visits and engagements, including here to the Welsh Parliament. (Senedd/Welsh Parliament)

As Queen Consort, The King's wife has continued to visit British military units and here she is hosted by the Queen's Own Gurkha Logistics Regiment. (MOD/Crown Copyright)

became more common, and she was invited to the Queen's Golden Jubilee celebrations in Buckingham Palace in 2002.

The couple's engagement was formally announced on February 10, 2005, and the wedding day was set for April 8, after securing the permission of his mother, the Prime Minister, and the Archbishop of Canterbury. As divorcees, the couple could not be married by the Church of England, so they had to opt for a civil service. This was the first time heir apparent – and the prospective head of the Church of England – had not been married by England's established Church.

In the meantime, Pope John Paul II died, and the Prince of Wales had to represent Queen Elizabeth II at his funeral in the Vatican. As a result, his second wedding was put back to April 9.

The Prince of Wales and Camilla were eventually married in the Guildhall, Windsor. They were joined by around 800 guests at a Service of Prayer and Dedication at St George's Chapel, Windsor Castle. The Service was followed by a reception at Windsor Castle hosted by Queen Elizabeth II. After her marriage, Camilla received the titles Duchess of Cornwall and Duchess of Rothesay, when in Scotland.

The Duchess has since become patron or president of over 90 charities, with a focus on

health and well-being, promoting literacy, the arts, animal welfare and supporting survivors of rape and sexual assault. The Duchess' mother and grandmother both died as a result of osteoporosis, so the Royal Osteoporosis Society was one of the first charities to receive her patronage, when she was appointed president

The Duchess of Cornwall accompanied her husband to the State Opening of Parliament in 2022. (Annabel Moeller/House of Lords)

in 2001.

She has also become involved in supporting units of the armed forces. The Duchess named the nuclear submarine HMS *Astute* in 2007, in front of a crowd of 10,000 spectators in Barrow-in-Furness. From 2007, the Duchess was Royal Colonel of the 4th Battalion, The Rifles regiment and became heavily involved in supporting members of the unit wounded in action in Iraq and Afghanistan. Her most high profile military engagement was the naming of the 65,000 ton aircraft carrier HMS *Prince of Wales* at Roysth dockyard in 2017. Royal Navy warships are rarely named by men these days, so the Prince of Wales did not name the vessel. The Duchess said the ship shared a title with her husband, adding: "So, I have a particular affection for it."

In 2016, Queen Elizabeth II passed on a number of patronages to other members of the royal family and, as part of this exercise, the Duchess of Cornwall assumed support for the children's charity Barnardo's, Battersea Dogs & Cats Home, and the Royal School of Needlework.

The Duchess' duties expanded after the passing of Queen Elizabeth II and her elevation to Queen Consort. She was appointed as a counsellor of state, allowing her to stand in for The King on official visits, ceremonial events or during minor illness. The Queen Consort is very much at the heart of the modern royal family. ●

PRINCE WILLIAM AND HIS FAMILY

A New Prince of Wales

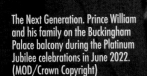

The Next Generation. Prince William and his family on the Buckingham Palace balcony during the Platinum Jubilee celebrations in June 2022. (MOD/Crown Copyright)

Prince William served as a Royal Air Force search and rescue helicopter pilot flying the Westland Sea King HAR3. (MOD/Crown Copyright)

At the heart of the British royal family is the concept of succession. Every monarch needs an heir apparent to be confident that the royal line is secure.

On June 21, 1982, William Arthur Philip Louis Windsor was born and so secured the line of succession of the House of Windsor.

In Britain, the heir apparent is traditionally titled Prince of Wales so when Queen Elizabeth II passed away Prince William stepped up to the title. Prince William's whole life has been focused on preparing him for the day he has to succeed his father as monarch.

In a big break from royal tradition, the young prince was educated at nursery and primary schools in London and Berkshire, before attending Eton in Windsor for his secondary schooling. There was no diversion to Gordonstoun for Prince William and his brother, Prince Harry. The two brothers, however, did receive personal tutoring in the summer holidays by a very young Rory Stewart, who has since achieved fame as a cabinet minister.

His studies were successful, with Prince William achieving an 'A' in geography, a 'C' in biology, and a 'B' in history of art in his A-Levels. On the back of this he secured a place at St Andrews University in Scotland in 2001 to study the history of art but, he subsequently switched to geography. As well graduating in 2005 with a 2:1 degree – a higher grade than achieved at university his father – the heir to the throne found the love of his life, Kate Middleton, during his time in St Andrews.

The following year, Prince William began army officer training at the Royal Military Academy Sandhurst and was subsequently commissioned into the Household Cavalry Regiment. After passing out from Sandhurst he moved to RAF Cranwell to begin training as a pilot and received his flying wings. Then he undertook a secondment to the Royal Navy, serving on the frigate HMS *Iron Duke*.

Unlike his brother, as heir to the throne Prince William could not be deployed to active war zones on security grounds so he was unable to join a unit that might be sent to Iraq or Afghanistan. A solution to the problem was for Prince William to serve as a Royal Air Force search and rescue pilot, flying the famous, yellow-painted Sea King helicopters. This gave him an important military role without running the risk of the heir apparent being put under threat from enemy action.

In 2009 he began his RAF helicopter pilot training and the following year he joined the search and rescue force at RAF Valley on the island of Anglesey, in Wales. He took part in his first rescue in October 2010, and conducted several more rescues over his next three years of military duty, including deployment to the Falkland Islands in the South Atlantic.

The same month as he began flying rescue missions from RAF Valley, Prince William proposed to Kate Middleton, rekindling the romance begun while students at St Andrews.

Kate was born a few months earlier than her husband and, unusually for a future wife of the heir apparent did not hail from an aristocratic family. Her parents had both previously worked for British Airways before setting up their own successful business.

The Duke and Duchess of Cambridge outside St Paul's Cathedral after the Platinum Jubilee service of thanksgiving for Queen Elizabeth II. (MOD/Crown Copyright)

The Duke and Duchess of Cambridge meet and greet during an official visit to Sweden. (Frankie Fouganthin)

The new Princess of Wales hosted sailors from HMS Prince of Wales in Buckingham Palace in September 2022. (MOD/Crown Copyright)

The Duke of Cambridge speaks at the United for Wildlife Transport Taskforce Meeting in 2017, as part of his engagement with organisations that aim to protection the environment. (Foreign and Commonwealth Office)

President Barack Obama and First Lady Michelle Obama talk with the Duke and Duchess of Cambridge at Buckingham Palace in May 2011 (Official White House Photo by Pete Souza)

"In 2017, Prince William stopped flying his air ambulance to concentrate full time on his royal duties, supporting his father and grandmother."

The royal couple's wedding took place at Westminster Abbey on April 29, 2011, complete with royal carriages, mounted guards, and celebrity guests. His grandmother appointed him the Duke of Cambridge to mark his wedding. The day was declared a public holiday and the event was broadcast live around the world. It's estimated that 35% of the British population tuned in to watch on television.

After the celebrations and a honeymoon on an Indian Ocean island, it was back to work at RAF Valley and the couple set up their first home in Wales.

Their first child, Prince George, was born on July 22, 2013, and his sister, Princess Charlotte, was born on May 2, 2015. Prince Louis was born on 23 April, 2018, to complete the new family.

Prince William retired from the RAF in 2013 but continued his involvement in emergency aviation by becoming a pilot with the East Anglian Air Ambulance, flying from Cambridge airport. During his time with the organisation, he was involved in recovering numerous seriously injured and sick patients.

In 2017, Prince William stopped flying his air ambulance to concentrate full time on his royal duties, supporting his father and grandmother.

When he'd turned 21, William had been appointed a councillor of state by Queen Elizabeth II so he was able to carry out royal duties on her behalf. After finishing university, he started to carry out royal visits in Britain and around the Commonwealth.

The regularity and profile of Prince William's royal duties intensified after his marriage, ranging from participating in events to welcome US President Barack Obama and his wife to the UK in 2011 to being ambassadors for the 2012 Olympic Games in London. When the G7 meeting of world leaders was held in Cornwall in June 2021, Prince William and his wife were part of the royal team hosting the distinguished guests.

As his grandmother's health declined, Prince William began to deputise for her in state occasions, such as accompanying his father to the State Opening of Parliament in May 2022. The Duchess of Cambridge also took on an

Prince George's official portrait to celebrate his ninth birthday. (Kensington Palace)

increasing royal role, undertaking visits and becoming the patron of various charities, with a focus on those involving issues surrounding young children, mental health, sport, addiction, and art.

The lives of the couple's three children have become increasingly public as they started school and pass other childhood milestones. Prince George accompanied his father, who is president of the England Football Association, to Wembley Stadium to watch the England vs Italy match during the Euro 2022 championship. The young prince's enthusiasm for the England team attracted extensive media coverage. His brother, Prince Louis, was the star of the Platinum Jubilee Pageant in June 2022, and his Royal Box hi-jinks with his sister captured national media attention.

Prince William played an important role in the ceremonial events to mark his grandmother's passing in September 2022, including participating in the funeral cortege to Westminster Hall and Westminster Abbey. He also stood vigil on Queen Elizabeth II in Westminster Hall with his brother and cousins. In the days leading up to the State Funeral, Prince William and his wife took part in a number of walkabouts to meet members of the public showing their respect to his grandmother.

After his grandmother's death, he took on the titles of Prince of Wales and Duke of Cornwall from this father. In the later role, Prince William is now one of the largest land owners in Britain and has direct role in the management of his estates and other properties. In November 2022, he visited Cardiff as Prince of Wales and was hosted by the Welsh Parliament or Senedd. In a break from the tradition established by his father, during the visit Prince William's spokesperson said that a new investiture is "not on the table." ●

The Princess Royal enjoying a day out in September 2021. (Ian Livesey)

PRINCESS ANNE

The Life of the Princess Royal

The Queen's second child, Anne Elizabeth Alice Louise, was born at Clarence House in London on August 15, 1950.

During her life, Princess Anne has blazed a trail for the royal family. Following a successful equestrian career she become the first royal Olympian, was voted BBC Sports Personality of the Year in 1971, became a member of the International Olympic Committee and was nominated for a Nobel Peace Prize. She was the first member of the modern royal family to remarry after being divorced.

As a young woman, the princess became an expert horsewoman winning an array of trophies and prizes. The pinnacle of her equestrian career was participation in the 1976 Montreal Olympics representing Great Britain in the three day event team. After suffering a collision, she had to remount half way around the course. The British team subsequently pulled out of the competition after two of its horses were injured.

As well as show jumping, she has also ridden winners in several horse races, including the Grand Military Steeplechase at Sandown Park and the Diamond Stakes at Royal Ascot. Subsequently, she pursued a career in sports administration as President of the British Olympic Association and became a member of the International Olympic Committee. She also played a leading role in London's successful bid to host the 2012 Olympic Games.

Her daughter Zara has followed her mother into a successful riding career. She won a silver medal at the London 2012 Olympics and was presented with her medal by her mother.

Anne was the first of Queen Elizabeth II's children to marry. She got married to army officer, Captain Mark Philips in November 1973, in a televised ceremony at Westminster Abbey. He was also a noted equestrian. Their children Peter and Zara were born in 1977 and 1981. Unusually, Captain Philips declined a royal title on his marriage and as a result his children with Anne do not have royal titles.

The royal couple made the headlines in March 1974, when they were the subject of a kidnap attempt in the Mall only a few hundred yards from Buckingham Palace. They were returning from a charity function when their car was forced off the road and a man waving a pistol tried to force them out of their vehicle. Their royal protection officer tried to intervene, but the bodyguard's gun jammed, and he was shot, leaving him seriously injured.

The kidnapper, Ian Ball, demanded Anne get out of the car so he could hold her for ransom, but she reportedly replied, "Not bloody likely!" as pedestrians and other police officers arrived on the scene. One, a former boxer, delivered a well aimed punch and floored Ball, which gave time for more police to apprehend the would be kidnapper.

In April 1992, Anne became the first of Queen Elizabeth II's children to divorce, and later that year married Tim Lawrence, a naval officer, at a ceremony in Scotland. The Church of Scotland allows divorcees to marry, unlike the Church of England at the time.

Since then, Anne has become one of the hardest working royals, being involved with more than 300 organisations and charities. In 2017, she topped the league table of working royals, clocking up 455 appearances at charity events, dinners, receptions, and other engagements around Britain, with a further 85 overseas events. Anne is often given sensitive tasks by the royal family and British government, so in 1990, she became the first member of the

> ## "In 1990, she was nominated for the Nobel Peace Prize as a result of her work on behalf of Save the Children."

royal family to make an official visit to the then USSR, as a guest of the Soviet government.

Her most high profile charity role has been as patron and president of the charity Save the Children, as well as being president and patron of Riding for the Disabled for more than 14 years. In 1990, she was nominated for the Nobel Peace Prize as a result of her work on behalf of Save the Children.

Although she never served in the armed force like her brothers, Princess Anne has accumulated dozens of honorary appointments in British and Commonwealth armed forces. She now takes her place on the Cenotaph every Remembrance Day with male members of the royal family. Her leading role in the events leading up to her mother's funeral last September added considerably to the Princess Royal's popularity.

During her life, Princess Anne has faced media criticism but has carved out a unique place in national life as a hard working and serious member of the royal family. ●

Although she never served in the military, the Princess Royal has strong affiliations with all the armed services. She married an army officer and later a naval commander, who was subsequently promoted to vice admiral. (MOD Crown Copyright)

Princess Anne and her husband, Vice Admiral Sir Timothy Laurence during a visit to the United States. (US Army Band)

Princess Anne in action at an Equestrian event in 1980. (Netherland National Archive)

Like mother, like daughter. Zara Phillips competed in the 2012 Olympics. (Henry Bucklow Lazy Photography/Sffubs)

EDWARD AND SOPHIE

The Duke and Duchess of Edinburgh

Prince Edward took on an increasing number of royal duties in the later years of Queen Elizabeth II's reign. (MOD Crown Copyright)

King Charles III's youngest brother, Edward, and his wife, Sophie, are now two of the hardest working members of the royal family.

Prince Edward was born in 1964 and as Queen Elizabeth II's fourth child, he never attracted the glamour and excitement of his older siblings. He appeared destined to follow his elder brother Andrew into the military when he enrolled at the Commando Training Centre at Lympstone in Devon in 1986. The intention was to train to become an officer in the Royal Marines, his father being captain general of them at the time. So, when he dropped out of his training course in January 1987, it created big headlines.

In a complete career change, Prince Edward declared it was his intention to become a theatrical impresario and ended up working for Andrew Lloyd Webber. His involvement with the royal version of the television programme It's A Knockout was less successful. In 1993, he founded Ardent Productions to make television documentaries about royal history. This ended badly when an Ardent television crew breached privacy guidelines by filming Prince William while he was a student at St Andrews University in 2002.

He married Sophie Helen Rhys-Jones in 1999 and they became the Earl and Countess of Wessex. In 2019, he also became the Earl of Forfar.

After winding up his business activities, Prince Edward began full time royal duties in support of his mother's Golden Jubilee celebrations. Edward and Sophie took on an extensive portfolio of charities and honorary military positions. He became heavily involved in lifting the burden from his grandfather for running the Duke of Edinburgh's Award scheme. His wife became a popular guest at military units, including visiting British troops in Afghanistan.

Over the next 20 years, the couple were often seen at Queen Elizabeth II's side at royal events. This culminated in the 2022 Platinum Jubilee celebrations, where Prince Edward and his wife played a prominent role. The King conferred the title of Duke of Edinburgh on his brother on his 59th birthday on March 9 this year. ●

Edward's wife, Sophie, was a popular visitor to the military units around the world, including here in Afghanistan at the height of Britain's involvement in the conflict in the central Asian country. (MOD Crown Copyright)

Prince Andrew served as a helicopter pilot in the Falklands conflict in 1982 and retained extensive links with the armed forces after his retirement. (US DoD)

PRINCE ANDREW

The Duke of York

King Charles III's younger brother, Prince Andrew, has gone from being one of the most popular members of the royal family in the 1980s to now having to withdraw from public life due to several scandals.

In the 1980s, Prince Andrew was the nation's most eligible bachelor. After his war service as a naval helicopter pilot during the 1982 Falklands conflict he was romantically linked by the media to a string of glamorous girlfriends.

In February 1986, he proposed to Sarah Ferguson, the red headed daughter of Major Ronald Ferguson. Soon Andrew's future wife was known to all as 'Fergie'. She was boisterous, fun loving and soon proved to be a tabloid headline writer's dream.

Andrew and Sarah were married at Westminster Abbey on July 23, 1986. The event was televised live and attracted a global audience of more than 500m. This was only two thirds of the audience for the wedding of Charles and Diana but still only 100m short of the audience for Neil Armstrong's first moon walk. On his marriage, Queen Elizabeth II granted Andrew the title Duke of York and his wife become the Duchess of York. However, the couple divorced in 1996.

After retiring from the Royal Navy in 2001, as a commander, he was made a special representative for international trade and investment for 10 years. This job was supposed to be about drumming up trade for British industry, but he was soon dubbed 'Air Miles Andy' by Fleet Street because of his VIP life style.

Prince Andrew's friendships with the disgraced US financier Jeffrey Epstein and the socialite Ghislaine Maxwell, as well as his disastrous attempts to explain his links to them in a 2019 interview with the BBC Newsnight television programme, led to Queen Elizabeth II ordering him to cease all official duties and give up his honorary military appointments. Subsequent legal issues make it unlikely that Prince Andrew will ever return to frontline royal duties. ●

Prince Andrew's daughters, Princesses Beatrice, and Eugenie, have taken on many of his royal duties since he has had to withdraw from public life. (Carfax2)

Controversy meant Prince Andrew had to stand down from his role as a trade envoy. (World Economic Forum)

DUKE OF YORK

Prince Harry set up the Invictus Games to allow disabled war veterans to take part in competitive sport. (MOD Crown Copyright)

PRINCE HARRY

The Duke of Sussex

The youngest son of King Charles III is now a global celebrity and has formally 'stepped back' from royal duties after taking up residence in California with his wife, Meghan Markle, and their two children, Archie, and Lilibet.

Henry Charles Albert David Windsor was born on September 15, 1984 and now carries the title Duke of Sussex but is universally known as Prince Harry. There is little the world does not know about Prince Harry's life after his book, Spare, was published in January 2023. It reportedly sold more than a million copies on its first day of publication, including 400,000 in Britain. As a result, there are few people who

don't have an opinion about Prince Harry.

Throughout his life Prince Harry has been in the media spotlight. Having one of the most glamorous women in the world as your mother

> **"Prince Harry returned to Britain to participate in the funerals of his grandfather and grandmother."**

and arguably the best known woman in the world as your grandmother meant there was little chance of him leading a normal life.

The very public separation and divorce of his parents in the 1990s added to the turmoil. After Princess Diana was killed in Paris in 1997 the 12 year old prince ended up playing a very public role in his mother's funeral. Harry, accompanied his father, brother, paternal grandfather Prince Philip and maternal uncle Charles Spencer, 9th Earl Spencer, in walking behind the funeral cortège from Kensington Palace to Westminster Abbey.

Unlike his father, Harry did not attend Gordonstoun School in Scotland and was sent to Eton in Windsor. He was awarded

Prince Harry's marriage in May 2018 to the American actress Meghan Markle was a major international media event. (Londisland)

On his return from his war service, Prince Harry became heavily involved in charity work for wounded military veterans. In 2014, he set up the Invictus Games to allow wounded service personnel from Britain and allied nations to compete against each other.

Prince Harry embarked on a new direction in his life when he married the American actress, Meghan Markle, in St George's Chapel in Windsor Castle on May 18, 2018. However, after the fairy-tale wedding the couple's life together clashed with the royal family and traditional protocols. In January 2020, Buckingham Palace announced that an agreement had been reached with Prince Harry for him "to step back from royal duties, including official military appointments." A year later it was announced that he would give up his position as captain general of the Royal Marines and hand back all the other honorary military appointments.

After first moving to Canada, Prince Harry and his wife bought a house in Montecito in California in June 2020. The couple have since pursued careers in the media and wellbeing sectors.

Prince Harry returned to Britain to participate in the funerals of his grandfather and grandmother, including standing vigil on Queen Elizabeth II as she lay in state in Westminster Hall. However, at the time of writing it is still not clear whether the couple will accept their invitation to his father's coronation. ●

two A-Levels in 2003. After a gap year spent in Australia and Lesotho, Prince Harry joined the British Army in 2005 and began training as an officer at the Royal Military Academy Sandhurst.

After being commissioned into the Household Cavalry Regiment, he was eventually deployed to Afghanistan in 2007 as a forward air controller, directing air strikes on Taliban positions. In 2008, Prince Harry transferred to the Army Air Corps and began training to fly Apache attack helicopters. Following a period of intense training on the complex aircraft, Prince Harry deployed with his squadron to Afghanistan in September 2012 for a six month tour of duty.

A young Prince Harry with his future sister-in-law, Kate Middleton, in 2008. (Nick Warner)

Prince Harry's service in Afghanistan led him to become involved in raising the profile of efforts to help veterans of the conflict. (US DoD)

PRINCESS BEATRICE

The eldest daughter of Prince Andrew was born in 1988. After working in the software and data industry, she married Edoardo Mapelli Mozzi, an Italian aristocrat and property developer in July 2020. After the death of Queen Elizabeth II, Princess Beatrice became a counsellor of state, allowing her to stand in for King Charles III for official duties, such as attending Privy Council meetings, signing routine documents, and receiving the credentials of new ambassadors.

PRINCESSES, DUKES,

The Wider Royal Family

PRINCESS ALEXANDRA

The late Queen Elizabeth II's cousin was one of the hardest working members of the royal family until illness led to her scaling back her commitments after 2013. At her peak, Princess Alexandra undertook more than 100 royal engagements each year and was a patron of dozens of charities. She married businessman Angus Ogilvy in 1963.

DUKE OF KENT

Prince Edward, Duke of Kent, is Queen Elizabeth II's oldest surviving cousin. As well as being related by way of his father, his mother was also a cousin of Prince Philip. After a 20 year career in the British Army, he embarked on a range of royal duties including acting as a trade envoy.

PRINCESS EUGENIE

The youngest daughter of Prince Andrew was born in March 2020 and after studying English literature and history of art at Newcastle University, she embarked on a career in the art sector. She married brand ambassador, Jack Brooksbank, in 2018 and the couple have since had two children.

DUKE OF GLOUCESTER

Prince Richard, Duke of Gloucester, is Queen Elizabeth II's youngest surviving cousin.
The Duke was born in 1944 and pursued a career as an architect. On the death of his father in 1974, he took on an increasing number of Royal duties.

AND SHOW JUMPERS

ZARAH TINDALL

The eldest daughter of the Princess Royal and her first husband, Captain Peter Phillips, is 20th in line to the throne after rules of succession were changed in 2011 to give equal weight to female children of royals. Her parents decided not to give Zarah and her brother, Peter, royal titles. Zarah is one of the highest profile younger royals both as an Olympic equestrian and through her marriage to the former England rugby union player and I am a Celebrity contestant, Mike Tindall.

THE LINE OF SUCCESSION

1. The Prince of Wales
2. Prince George of Wales
3. Princess Charlotte of Wales
4. Prince Louis of Wales
5. The Duke of Sussex
6. Master Archie Mountbatten-Windsor
7. Miss Lilibet Mountbatten-Windsor
8. The Duke of York
9. Princess Beatrice, Mrs Edoardo Mapelli Mozzi
10. Miss Sienna Mapelli Mozzi
11. Princess Eugenie, Mrs Jack Brooksbank
12. Master August Brooksbank
13. The Earl of Wessex
14. Viscount Severn
15. The Lady Louise Mountbatten-Windsor
16. The Princess Royal
17. Mr Peter Phillips
18. Miss Savannah Phillips
19. Miss Isla Phillips
20. Zarah, Mrs Michael Tindall
21. Miss Mia Tindall
22. Miss Lena Tindall
23. Master Lucas Tindall

Source: Buckingham Palace

ROYAL DUTIES

Prince Charles' Long Apprenticeship

Queen Elizabeth II's long life meant that Charles had a lengthy apprenticeship before assuming his duties as monarch. (@RoyalFamily)

Queen Elizabeth II hosted world leaders for the D-Day 75th Anniversary commemorations in 2019 and was assisted by the then Prince of Wales. (White House)

It is famously said that being the Prince of Wales – the male heir to the British throne - does not have a formal job description. The holder of the ancient title has to forge their own role.

Since his birth in 1948, Charles had been set to be King one day and his early life was mapped out by his parents to prepare him for his future role. He attended Gordonstoun public school to develop his character, was invested as Prince of Wales to signal his connection to the Principality, attended school in Australia to bolster links with the Commonwealth, and served in the armed forces to establish his credentials ahead of becoming their commander-in-chief. Then, of course, he was expected to marry and produce his own heir.

By the 1990s, as he entered middle age the Prince of Wales was clearly no longer an 'apprentice King'. By the turn of the century, he had become a senior member of the royal family, and he knew his own mind. When Queen Elizabeth, The Queen Mother and Princess Margaret both passed away in 2002, the royal family underwent a generational change. The Prince of Wales had to step up and take on an increasing burden of state duties from his mother and father, who were now in their seventies and suffered from series of health scares. He was no longer the 'heir in training' but the 'monarch in waiting'.

A major milestone was his marriage in 2005 to Mrs Camilla Parker-Bowles. This ended more than 30 years of instability in the Prince of Wales's life. The public reconciliation of Prince William and Prince Harry with their new stepmother, added to the impression that an important page had been turned.

The Prince of Wales had long been entrusted with foreign visits to sensitive locations and he became a trail blazer into unfamiliar territory for the royal family. He was the first royal ever to visit the Republic of Ireland on official business, when he crossed the Irish Sea in 1996.

His next high profile mission was to represent his mother at the formal handover of Hong Kong to Chinese sovereignty in 1997. This event was loaded with end of Empire symbolism, complete with the lowering of the Union Flag and the Prince of Wales, alongside the last British governor of Hong Kong, Chris Patten, boarding HMY *Britannia* to sail off into the South China Sea. At the rain soaked handover, The Prince of Wales read Queen Elizabeth II's message to Hong Kong residents, which said: "Britain is part of Hong Kong's history and Hong Kong is part of Britain's history. We are also part of each other's future."

The handover ceremonies went smoothly. Everyone played their part as per the carefully choreographed script, agreed after tortuous negotiations between the Beijing communist government and the British Foreign Office. The Prince of Wales looked the part and did his duty. He was now the royal family's 'go to guy' for sensitive missions.

When Polish-born Pope John Paul II passed away in 2005, after 27 years a pontiff, it was no surprise that the Prince Wales was dispatched to represent Britain at his funeral. The importance of his participation in this globally significant event was such that the Prince of Wales had to delay his wedding by a day.

After the turn of the century, the Prince of Wales was dubbed the 'hardest-working member of the royal family', on account of his packed diary of official engagements and visits. These ran to 560 official engagements in 2008, 499 in 2010, and more than 600 in 2011.

One of Queen Elizabeth II's proudest achievements was the growth and flourishing of

The then Prince of Wales increasingly assumed duties from Queen Elizabeth II, particularly those involving short notice engagements overseas. Here he talks to rescue workers in the aftermath of Hurricane Katrina in the USA in 2005. (FEMA)

Over the years The King has seen Britain's political leaders come and go. Here in 2011 a young Boris Johnson, then mayor of London, waits to meet the then Prince of Wales, (MOD Crown Copyright)

During the COVID-19 pandemic in 2020 Queen Elizabeth II took up residence in her home in Windsor Castle and like everyone else conducted official business over Zoom. (New Zealand Government)

> ## "A major milestone was his marriage in 2005 to Mrs Camilla Parker-Bowles. This ended more than 30 years of instability in the Prince of Wales's life."

the Commonwealth as Britain retreated from its Empire in the 1950s and 1960s. By the time of her passing in 2022, the Commonwealth had 56 members, almost all of which were former British colonies. The organisation, formally known as the Commonwealth of Nations, now includes four nations, Gabon, Rwanda, Togo, and Mozambique, that had no previous links to Britain or its Empire.

For much of her life, Queen Elizabeth II travelled across the Commonwealth making a concerted effort to attend the organisation's head of government meetings, often putting her at odds with the London government. She also made a point of trying to be present to open the Commonwealth Games, which was the organisation's flagship sporting and cultural event.

So as her capability to travel for prolonged periods declined, Queen Elizabeth II passed over many Commonwealth related duties to her eldest son. It gave him experience of working with the organisation and its leaders. It was also to build support for his taking over as head of the Commonwealth after her death. The position as head of the Commonwealth is not linked to the hereditary British monarchy, so it succession is dependent on the goodwill and support of the organisation's heads of government and their populations.

The Prince of Wales stepped into his mother's shoes for the Commonwealth Games opening duty in 2010, when he travelled to New Delhi to open the event. Three years later he represented her for the first time at a Commonwealth Heads of Government Meeting, in Colombo, Sri

Lanka. When the organisation's leaders meet in London in April 2018, Queen Elizabeth II proposed that her son would succeed her. At an event in Buckingham Palace to welcome the Commonwealth leaders, she said: "It is my sincere wish that the Commonwealth will continue to offer stability and continuity for future generations, and will decide that one day the Prince of Wales should carry on the important work started by my father in 1949." The following day the meeting agreed that its next head would be the Prince of Wales.

When Queen Elizabeth II passed her 80th birthday attention increasingly focused on how the Prince of Wales would conduct himself after his accession to the throne. Some politicians and media commentators expressed concern that his high profile role in support of his favoured causes would prevent him fulfilling his duties as monarch in a truly impartial way. The Guardian newspaper staged a high profile legal claim under the Freedom of Information Act to gain access to the famous 'black spider memos' that the Prince of Wales had dispatched to government ministers. In 2015, the Supreme Court ordered the Cabinet Office to release the documents. However, when they were published the reaction was rather underwhelming and many media commentators wondered what the fuss had all been about.

The Prince of Wales was able to celebrate his

eldest son's wedding in 2011 and subsequent birth of his first grandson, Prince George, in 2013. He'd watched his youngest son, Prince Harry, head off to war in Afghanistan as an Army Air Corps helicopter pilot in 2012. Then Harry married the American actress, Meghan Markle, in 2018. A family crisis ensued in early 2020 when Prince Harry and his wife decided to step back from royal duties. The event dominated media coverage of the royal family at the time, but within weeks it was overshadowed by the COVID-19 pandemic.

As Britain was closed down by government-ordered lock-downs in a bid to contain the virus, contingency plans were put into action to protect the royal family and ensure continuity of the royal succession. Queen Elizabeth II and her husband relocated to Windsor Castle to live in a closely controlled bubble. The Prince of Wales and his wife moved to Birkhall on the Balmoral Estate and Prince William and his family isolated at Anmar Hall on the Sandringham Estate.

This caution was justified when the Prince of Wales tested positive on March 25, 2020, and had to self-isolate at Birkhall while he recovered from mild symptoms. His wife tested negative. This was in the first wave of the pandemic when there was concern the virus was spreading out of control. Two days later, Prime Minister Boris Johnson was taken seriously ill with the virus ➲

The then Prince of Wales represented Queen Elizabeth II during the ceremony in November 2021 to mark the Caribbean island of Barbados transition to a republic. (PMO Barbados)

Prince William also joined the royal family's effort to take the strain of official duties off Queen Elizabeth II during her later years. (MOD Crown Copyright)

In July 2022 Queen Elizabeth II carried out one of her final in-person official visits to open the Thames Hospice, accompanied by her daughter, The Princess Royal. (@ RoyalFamily)

and rushed to hospital. It subsequently emerged that soon after this Prince William had also tested positive and was 'very ill' at home.

Royal business was now conducted largely over the internet using Zoom meetings, but Queen Elizabeth II reportedly quickly got the hang of the new technology and was soon happily speaking to world leaders and others on her computer every day. As the pandemic was at its peak in April, the monarch made a moral boosting broadcast to the nation. It was watched by an estimated 24m viewers in Britain. She invoked the wartime spirit, when she asked Britons to "take comfort that while we may have more still to endure, better days will return; we will be with our friends again; we will be with our families again; we will meet again."

Queen Elizabeth II was keen to do more in a time of national crisis and personally knighted the 100-year-old charity fundraiser Captain Tom Moore in the grounds of Windsor Castle in a special ceremony in July 2020.

In another move to bolster public morale and ensure take up of the COVID-19 vaccine, the monarch announced in January 2021 that along with her husband she had received the jab. The Prince of Wales and his wife received their vaccines the following month.

As the impact of the pandemic abated, the royal family began to return to in-person public duties, with the Prince of Wales and his wife in the forefront of visits to thank key workers for their services at the height of the outbreak.

The royal family was hit by tragedy in April 2021, when Prince Philip passed away at Windsor Castle. Queen Elizabeth II travelled to her final state opening of Parliament in May 2021, but her health was declining and later in the summer started to appear in public using a walking stick. The monarch's appearance at a series of events in the autumn, the COP26 summit in Glasgow and the National Service of Remembrance, had to be cancelled after a brief stay in hospital. The Prince of Wales stood in for his mother at both events.

In November 2021, the Prince of Wales attended the ceremonies held to mark the transition of Barbados into a parliamentary republic, which removed his mother as Barbadian head of state. He was invited by Prime Minister Mia Mottley as the future head of the Commonwealth, and it was the first time that a member of the royal family attended the transition of a realm to a republic. ●

In May 2022 the then Prince of Wales stood in for his mother during the opening of Parliament and read her Queen's Speech outlining the government's programme. (House of Lords)

THE DUKE OF EDINBURGH'S PASSING

An End of an Era

As an accomplished pilot, it was fitting that the Royal Air Force aerobatic team, the famous Red Arrows, flew over Windsor Castle during the funeral in tribute to the Duke of Edinburgh. (MOD Crown Copyright)

The Duke of Edinburgh carried out his final public engagement in August 2017, with his last parade as captain general of the Royal Marines outside Buckingham Palace. (Royal Pool, Getty Images)

On April 9, 2021, Prince Philip, Duke of Edinburgh passed away quietly at Windsor Castle with his wife of more than 73 years and other members of the royal family present.

The death of the longest serving royal consort was followed by an outpouring of public sympathy for Queen Elizabeth II and her family. During his long life, the Duke was a constant at his wife's side on her many official engagements and royal tours. He won praise for largely inventing the role of royal consort and sacrificing his own naval career to support Queen Elizabeth II in her royal duties. In the 21st century this is seen as unremarkable but, in 1950s Britain this was a new departure and ground breaking.

Despite being married to the monarch and having a very constrained royal role, the Duke was able to forge his own distinctive public role. The Duke was passionate about the environment, science and technology, the welfare of Britain's servicemen and women, and encouraging young people to fulfil their potential. He was always looking for ways to employ his position to benefit his causes and interests. His creation of the Duke of Edinburgh's Award Scheme will be a lasting legacy and illustrated how he was able to use his celebrity to influence British national life, without overstepping the bounds and constraints of his royal role.

Between 1952 and his retirement from official duties in August 2017, aged 96, he completed 22,219 solo engagements. During his life he was the patron of more than 800 charities and organisations, as well as having some 17 honorary military decorations and appointments in 48 countries.

Throughout his life, the Duke was highly active, including being a competitive polo player

The Duke of Edinburgh organised many details of his own funeral, including designing and building the unique Land Rover that carried his coffin. (MOD Crown Copyright)

and then a carriage driver. A major interest was flying, and he learned to pilot both fixed wing aircraft and helicopters. After 44 years as a pilot, he retired in August 1997 with 5,986 hours spent in 59 different aircraft. He even found time to become an accomplished painter and yachtsman.

However, he was famously undiplomatic and, on several occasions, got caught up in media and diplomatic storms over alleged gaffes. But during his life, the media and public came to value the Duke's 'authenticity'. He may have regularly been criticised for speaking his mind or making bad taste jokes – often at his own expense - but over time he was increasingly respected for actually having an opinion and not taking his life too

seriously. In an address to the General Dental Council in 1960, he jokingly coined a new word, saying: "Dontopedalogy is the science of opening your mouth and putting your foot in it, a science which I have practised for a good many years."

He reached some major royal milestones during his life including becoming the longest-serving British royal consort in 2009, the oldest-ever male British royal in February 2013, as well as being the third-longest-lived member of the royal family after Queen Elizabeth, Queen Mother, who reached 101 in 2002, and Princess Alice, Duchess of Gloucester, who died aged 102 in 2004.

During his old age, the Duke suffered from a

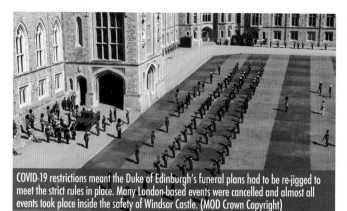

COVID-19 restrictions meant the Duke of Edinburgh's funeral plans had to be re-jigged to meet the strict rules in place. Many London-based events were cancelled and almost all events took place inside the safety of Windsor Castle. (MOD Crown Copyright)

COVID-19 restrictions meant many of aspects of the Duke of Edinburgh's funeral had to be modified, including the wearing of face masks by many participants. (MOD Crown Copyright)

Representatives of all of Britain's armed services lined the route to St George's Chapel inside Windsor Castle. (MOD Crown Copyright)

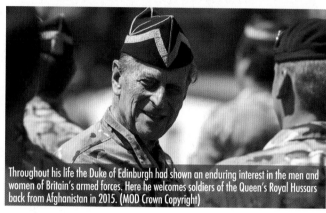

Throughout his life the Duke of Edinburgh had shown an enduring interest in the men and women of Britain's armed forces. Here he welcomes soldiers of the Queen's Royal Hussars back from Afghanistan in 2015. (MOD Crown Copyright)

series of illnesses and health scares but always remained publicly cheerful and stoic using his self deprecating sense of humour to make light of his increasing infirmity, telling one journalist in 2000 that "bits of me are falling off already."

Even in his 90s the Duke was reluctant to retire from royal duties, despite having a cardiothoracic stent fitted in 2011. His increasing frailty was highlighted during the 2012 Diamond Jubilee celebrations when he had to be hospitalised for five days.

He was determined to go out in style and strode outside Buckingham Palace in August 2017 for his final solo engagement to hand over the reigns as captain general of the Royal Marines.

The following year he received a hip replacement and spent more time in hospital. In 2019 he was involved in a car accident while driving near the Sandringham Estate and then voluntarily gave up his driving licence.

During the COVID-19 pandemic in March 2020, Queen Elizabeth II and the Duke moved to Windsor Castle to live. They reduced their engagements and lived quietly. In early 2021, the Duke was admitted to hospital on two occasions. Sadly, two months short of his 100th

A bearer party of Royal Marines carry the Duke of Edinburgh into the St George VI Chapel in Windsor for the final time. (MOD Crown Copyright)

"Dontopedalogy is the science of opening your mouth and putting your foot in it, a science which I have practised for a good many years."

birthday, the Duke of Edinburgh passed away quietly in his sleep, with "old age" reportedly being recorded as his official cause of death by Sir Huw Thomas, the head of the Royal Medical Household.

Once the news of the Duke's death was announced, plans for his funeral and a period of national mourning swung into action. The BBC and other broadcasters interrupted their television and radio programming. There were gun salutes across the UK, Gibraltar and on Royal Navy ships at sea. Flags were flown at half mast, bells were rung in Westminster Abbey, parliament paused passing new laws during the period of mourning and sporting events held pauses as a mark of respect. COVID-19 restrictions meant the public were asked not to gather outside royal residences or leave flowers.

The Duke was famously an unsentimental

and practical man, and it was no surprise when it emerged that he had planned almost every aspect of his funeral, even down to helping design a special Land Rover hearse to bear his coffin. Due to the public health guidelines, some elements of the plan had been modified, although the day was still very much in line with the Duke's wishes.

His funeral was a ceremonial royal funeral, rather than a state funeral, which are reserved for monarchs.

On Saturday April 17, at 2.40pm, the coffin emerged from the State Entrance of Windsor Castle into the Quadrangle. The Procession moved towards St George's Chapel, through Engine Court, Chapel Hill Parade Ground and into Horseshoe Cloister, arriving at the West Steps. The procession route was lined by representatives from the Royal Navy, the Royal Marines, the 4th Battalion Royal Regiment of Scotland and the Royal Air Force. Minute Guns were fired by The King's Troop Royal Horse Artillery from the East Lawn of Windsor Castle for the duration of the procession and the Curfew Tower Bell tolled.

Senior members of the royal family followed the coffin on foot before the bearer party of Royal Marines carried it up the west steps of the chapel before pausing for a national minutes silence.

Inside, perhaps the most poignant moment of the day occurred as Queen Elizabeth II, dressed in black, had to sit alone because of the COVID-19 restrictions.

During the service, a small choir of four sang pieces of music chosen by the Duke of Edinburgh. The funeral service was conducted by the Dean of Windsor and lasted for approximately 50 minutes, and, at its conclusion, the Duke of Edinburgh's coffin was lowered into the royal vault. ●

A RIGHT ROYAL CELEBRATION

Summer of the Platinum Jubilee

Royal generations. Queen Elizabeth II made her last Buckingham Palace balcony appearance during the Jubilee celebrations in June 2022, alongside the future King and his eldest son's family. (MOD Crown Copyright)

In June 2022, Britain celebrated Queen Elizabeth II's Platinum Jubilee with events in London and across the country as well as the Commonwealth. No other British monarch had served 70 years on the throne, so it was intended to be a very special occasion.

The events of the summer proved to be the last time Queen Elizabeth II was able to participate in large scale public events. Her frailty was now obvious, and she had to miss a number of events, particularly those that lasted a long time.

To mark the anniversary a four day bank holiday weekend was declared in the UK to provide what Buckingham Palace described as "an opportunity for communities and people throughout the United Kingdom to come together to celebrate the historic milestone."

A series of events got underway in January 2022, and continued through into the summer, culminating in the four day celebration weekend centred in and around London.

During May the 2022 renewal of the annual Royal Windsor Horse Show at Windsor Castle, was titled A Gallop Through History, and concluded with a 90-minute celebration in tribute to Queen Elizabeth II. It featured 500 horses and 1,000 dancers, with various members of the royal family, including the Duke and

Duchess of Gloucester, the Earl and Countess of Wessex, and the Princess Royal in attendance. Queen Elizabeth II attended on May 15 and visibly enjoyed the entertainment. The Queen's youngest granddaughter, Lady Louise Mountbatten-Windsor, drove in the carriage that once belonged to her grandfather, the Duke of Edinburgh, and had been featured in his funeral. Actors Helen Mirren and Tom Cruise were also involved, with Mirren playing the part of Queen Elizabeth I.

The celebration weekend kicked off on Thursday June 2 in London with Queen Elizabeth II's traditional Birthday Parade, which is also known as Trooping the Colour. This saw

> "People were invited to share friendship, food and fun with neighbours as part of the Platinum Jubilee celebrations," said the Palace.

over 1,400 parading soldiers, 200 horses and 400 musicians marching down the Mall from Buckingham Palace and culminated with the traditional RAF flypast, watched by members of the royal family from the Buckingham Palace balcony.

In the evening, the first of more than 3,500 flaming beacons were lit in a special ceremony at Windsor Castle by Queen Elizabeth II, who touched a glittering globe to light the principal beacon. Her grandson, Prince William oversaw the lighting of the Tree of Trees in Buckingham Palace. This was followed by the remainder of the beacons throughout the United Kingdom, Channel Islands, Isle of Man and UK Overseas Territories, as well as for the first time in each of the capital cities of the Commonwealth.

On Friday June 3, a Service of Thanksgiving for Queen Elizabeth II's reign was held at St Paul's Cathedral. The Queen had hoped to attend but Buckingham Palace said she was feeling some "discomfort" after attending the Trooping the Colour parade so missed the event.

Similarly, the following day, The Queen had hoped to indulge her great passion for horse racing by attending the Derby on Epsom Downs, but was still feeling unwell so watched the races on television. During the evening a

The then Prince of Wales and his son, Prince William, went to Parliament in May 2022 to deputise for Queen Elizabeth II to mark the opening of the parliamentary session. (MOD Crown Copyright)

special live concert from outside Buckingham Palace brought together some of the world's biggest entertainment stars to celebrate the most significant and joyous moments from Queen Elizabeth II's seven decade reign in an event titled the "Platinum Party at the Palace".

In a surprise for the crowds and television audiences at home, The Queen had filmed a comedy sketch with the animated film character Paddington Bear. Following in the tradition of her iconic 2012 Olympic parachuting skit, she told the Peruvian bear and Britain's most famous illegal immigrant that she also kept a marmalade sandwich in her handbag 'for later'.

Across the nation on Sunday June 5, communities were encouraged to join in the Big Lunch. Buckingham Palace said the idea was to "bring the Jubilee celebrations into the heart of every community" and to allow them "to celebrate their connections and get to know each other a little bit better."

"People were invited to share friendship, food and fun with neighbours as part of the Platinum Jubilee celebrations," said the Palace. The UK's longest ever street party was held in Morecambe in Lancashire, where 500 tables were set up over a distance of 2.6km.

In central London, the Platinum Jubilee Pageant saw performers, dancers, musicians, military personnel, key workers, and volunteers unite to tell the story of Queen Elizabeth II's 70 year reign in a festival of creativity. The celebration combined pomp and ceremony, street arts, theatre, music, circus, and costumes, as well as cutting-edge visual technology, drawing on talent from every part of the United Kingdom and across the Commonwealth. The procession was led by a military parade comprised of units and personnel drawn from

Queen Elizabeth II saw off the baton on its journey to the 2022 Commonwealth Games in Birmingham in October 2021, via 72 Commonwealth countries and territories. (@ RoyalFamily)

across the realms.

Forming an important part of the event, the 'River of Hope' section comprised 200 silk flags which processed down The Mall and appeared like a moving river. Primary and secondary school children created pictures of their hopes and aspirations for the planet over the next 70 years. A selection of these creations were transferred on to silk flags, which were carried by secondary school pupils.

The pageant included a cavalcade of vintage vehicles from each of the decades of the monarch's reign, carrying sporting, entertainment and other celebrities from each era. It was unofficially dubbed the 'parade of national treasures'.

Again, The Queen chose not to be present in the official viewing stand, but the crowds were not disappointed. They were entertained by young Prince Louis, pulling funny faces and getting very excited by the show, much to his parents displeasure.

At the close of the festivities, Queen Elizabeth

Queen Elizabeth stole the show ahead of the Platinum Jubilee Party in the Park with her TV appearance alongside Britain's favourite bear, Paddington. (@ RoyalFamily)

II delighted the hundreds of thousands of people in the Mall by making an appearance on the balcony of Buckingham Palace. She was accompanied by the Prince of Wales and his wife, along with Prince William and his family. It was a powerful symbol of royal continuity, and it would prove to be her last ever appearance on the famous balcony. She later issued a statement in which she thanked everyone for their "good wishes."

His mother's frailty meant the Prince of Wales, along with other senior royals, took a leading role in many of the Platinum Jubilee celebrations. This trend had accelerated earlier in the year. Queen Elizabeth II attended the service of thanksgiving for Prince Philip at Westminster Abbey on March 29, but was unable to make it to the Commonwealth Day service that month as well as the royal Maundy service in April.

In a major departure from tradition, she missed the State Opening of Parliament in May 2022, for the first time in 59 years. She had been absent from this major ceremonial event, ➲

Important events of the Queen's reign were celebrated during the Jubilee Pageant, which involved thousands of members of the public and a 'parade of national treasure' celebrities. (MOD Crown Copyright)

which formally launches the parliamentary calendar, back in 1959 and 1963, when she was pregnant with Prince Andrew and Prince Edward, respectively. The Prince of Wales and the Duke of Cambridge stood in for her, in their capacity as counsellors of state.

The year was full of milestones for Queen Elizabeth II. She became the second-longest reigning monarch in history among those whose exact dates of reign are known. On 13 June, she reached 70 years and 127 days on the throne, surpassing King Bhumibol Adulyadej of Thailand. Only Louis XIV of France - - who became king at the age of four in 1643 - reigned for longer.

On July 15, 2022, Queen Elizabeth II conducted her last ever public appearance when she formally opened a new 28-bed facility at Thames Hospice close to Windsor Castle. She had first opened Thames Hospice in November 1987 and this was her fourth visit to the charity. Accompanied by the Princess Royal, the monarch met and chatted to volunteers, staff and one of the patients, Pat White.

During the summer of 2022, the monarch's health deteriorated further and she was unable to play a role in any of the celebrations

Queen Elizabeth II travelled to Edinburgh in June 2022 to participate in her final royal week event in Scotland. (MOD Crown Copyright)

As per tradition, troops of the Household Division accompanied the monarch's representatives to the opening of the parliamentary session in May 2022. (MOD Crown Copyright)

The armed forces had a prominent role in the Jubilee Pageant down the Mall. (MOD Crown Copyright)

surrounding the Commonwealth Games held in Birmingham.

Later in the summer, Queen Elizabeth II made her traditional journey to the Balmoral Estate in Scotland for her summer holiday. She received visits from many family and friends who reported that she still remained mentally sharp, even though the 96-year-old was becoming more frail. The summer was a period of great political instability after Boris Johnson resigned as prime minister on July 7. All through the summer the Conservative Party conducted a leadership election to choose his successor. It meant Queen Elizabeth II had to be on alert to perform her constitutional duty to ask the winner of the leadership election to form a government and take over as prime minister.

This process finally concluded on September 5 when Liz Truss was declared the winner and would soon be Queen Elizabeth II's 15th prime minister. Due to the monarch's frailty, it was decided that the transition of political power would take place in Balmoral Castle rather than Buckingham Palace. It was the first time the event had taken place outside London. As a result Johnson had to head to Balmoral on the following morning for his final audience with

Queen Elizabeth II. Close behind, flying on a separate aircraft was Truss who was ushered in to see the monarch a few minutes later in the time honoured fashion.

By tradition, the details of royal audiences are highly confidential but Johnson later commented: "The last audience I had with her –

The then Prince of Wales officiated at the closing ceremony of the Commonwealth Games in August 2022. (@ RoyalFamily)

one of the reasons why it was so shocking to hear about her death was because, in that audience, she had been absolutely on it just two days before her death. And she was actively focused on geopolitics, on UK politics, quoting statesmen from the 50s – it was quite extraordinary."

He said she "seem[ed] well", and added: "She seemed very bright, very focused – look, I'm – she was clearly not well. And that was the thing that I found so moving when I – we – all heard about her death two days later. I just thought how incredible that her sense of duty had kept her going in the way that it had."

The following day, the monarch had been due to attend an online meeting of the Privy Council to swear in new ministers in Truss's government, but she was advised to rest by doctors, so the event was cancelled. Queen Elizabeth II's final public statement was issued later on September 7, sending her condolences to the victims of a mass stabbing incident in Saskatchewan in Canada.

Overnight, Queen Elizabeth II's health declined rapidly, and her family were alerted that they should prepare for the worst and head to Balmoral. By 3pm on September 8, 2022 she passed away and Britain had a new King. ●

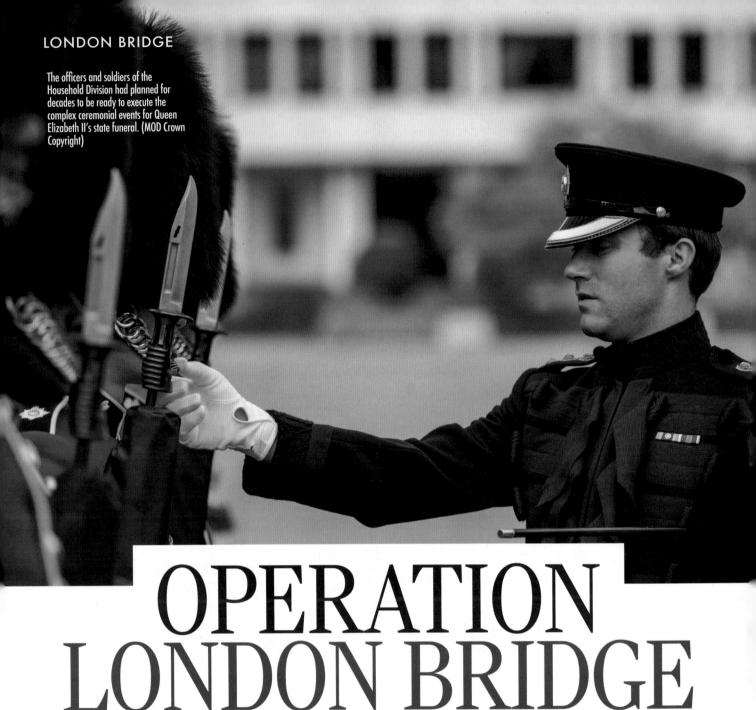

The officers and soldiers of the Household Division had planned for decades to be ready to execute the complex ceremonial events for Queen Elizabeth II's state funeral. (MOD Crown Copyright)

OPERATION LONDON BRIDGE

The Queen is Dead, Long Live the King

Almost as soon as a British monarch is crowned, royal courtiers and government officials begin planning for the day their heir has to succeed them. It is called 'continuity of government' in Whitehall parlance. Without a monarch, the British state would lack legal authority – judges need to have to authority to send criminals to jail, soldiers need to receive legal orders from their officers and taxes can only be raised by the monarch's tax collectors. So, as soon as a monarch passes away, the machinery of the British state has to be ready to swing into action to ensure the immediate accession of the new monarch to the throne.

The original phrase was translated from the French phrase, 'Le roi est mort, vive le roi'. This, in turn, is derived from the law of 'le mort saisit le vif' - that the transfer of sovereignty occurs instantaneously upon the moment of death of the previous monarch. In the Middle Ages, French was the primary language of the

Wellington Barracks was the nerve centre of Operation London Bridge and the site of the London Military Operations Centre, which co-ordinated he ceremonial events with the capital's police and other emergency services. (MOD Crown Copyright)

At the heart of Operation London Bridge was a state funeral involving thousands of military personnel, wearing their full ceremonial uniforms. It was a major logistic exercise get all the right kit in the right place. (MOD Crown Copyright)

nobility in England, and the proclamation was quickly taken up as ideally representing the same tradition—which in England dates back to 1272, when Henry III died while his son, Edward I, was fighting in the Crusades. To avoid any chance of a war erupting over the order of succession, the Royal Council proclaimed: "The throne shall never be empty; the country shall never be without a monarch." Thus, Edward was declared king immediately, and he reigned in absentia until news of his father's death reached him and he returned to England.

Within Buckingham Palace and Whitehall senior officials were responsible for preparing for the day Queen Elizabeth II passed away, under the code name Operation London Bridge. Contingency plans for every eventually were prepared so as soon as doctors pronounced on the passing of Queen Elizabeth II, the machinery of state would be put in motion.

The brutal reality for the new monarch is that as soon he became King, there was state business to execute. He had simultaneously to oversee the funeral of his mother, comfort his family and become head of state. To make this process as easy as possible, a huge part of Operation London Bridge contingency planning was underway to preparing the way for Queen Elizabeth II's state funeral. The late Queen and her husband, Prince Philip, were closely involved in this planning and laid out their wishes for how they wanted it to unfold. While many elements of the funeral of a British monarch follow ancient tradition, Queen Elizabeth II made some specific requests. She, for example, is believed to have set out the plans for her to lay in state in St Giles Cathedral in Edinburgh if she passed away in Scotland.

The then Prince of Wales, was likewise closely involved in the elements of London Bridge concerning his accession to the throne. Tradition called for the beginning of a new reign to be proclaimed around Britain, but many new and innovative features were developed for the plans to proclaim King Charles III's accession.

A large part of the London Bridge planning was developing the procedures to announce the news and organise media coverage of the accession and week of mourning for Queen Elizabeth II. The BBC, ITV and other British broadcasters were closely involved in the planning so they could rapidly begin broadcast coverage. The dawn of the internet age meant that London Bridge plans had to be adopted to ensure the events were live streamed online, social media feeds were updated and details of how the public could show their respects to the late Queen were widely distributed.

Royal traditions may have ancient roots, but Operation London Bridge planners had to ensure the historic events they were about to oversee were fit for the 21st century. ●

Every aspect of Queen Elizabeth II's state funeral was rehearsed with military precision so the troops of the Household Division were ready to go once news was announced that their monarch had passed away. (MOD Crown Copyright)

As garrison sergeant major of London District, Warrant Officer 1 Andrew "Vern" Stokes (left), played a leading role in the planning for the funeral of Queen Elizabeth II. (MOD Crown Copyright)

GOD SAVE THE KING

September 8, 2022

After Queen Elizabeth II's doctors told her to rest on September 7, concerns started growing about the 96-year-old monarch's health. Her eldest son was at Dumfries House in Ayrshire attending an international symposium on allergies. Early on the morning of September 8 he was collected by the royal, burgundy-liveried, helicopter and flown to Balmoral, arriving just after 10.30am.

His sister and wife were already at the royal family's Highland estate amid worries that Queen Elizabeth II's condition was serious. Other members of the royal family were notified and began preparing to travel to Royal Deeside and they arrived later in the afternoon. In London, government ministers and officials were alerted to the situation. Just after midday, Buckingham Palace issued a statement expressing concern for the monarch's health. The Speaker of the House of Commons, Sir Lindsay Hoyle made a brief statement of good wishes to Queen Elizabeth II from the speaker's chair, live on television. The BBC and other broadcasters started their rolling coverage of the story. It was becoming apparent to viewers that the situation was serious and momentous events were unfolding before them.

It was only a few hours later that Queen Elizabeth II passed away. Her official death

> **"Royal footmen followed tradition by posting a notice on an easel near the gates of Buckingham Palace. It simply stated that "The Queen died peacefully at Balmoral this afternoon."**

certificate gave the time of death as 3.10pm and recorded the cause, just as 'old age'. The Princess Royal was recorded as registering her mother's death.

At that moment Britain had a new monarch.

The Prime Minister, Liz Truss was notified at 4.30pm, and minutes later, Operation London Bridge was formally activated. Across government, wheels started to be put in motion for when the nation and the world would be formally told the news of Queen Elizabeth II's passing. The BBC and other broadcasters were alerted to be ready. The formal notice was issued just after 6.30pm and the newsreader Hugh Edwards broke the news on the BBC within minutes. Normal programming was suspended and tributes started to be broadcast.

Flags on public buildings, including Buckingham Palace and 10 Downing Street, as well as on Royal Navy ships were lowered. At Balmoral Castle the Royal Standard was lowered and then raised again, as the new King was present. Royal footmen followed tradition by posting a notice on an easel near the gates

Flags were lowered on royal palaces and government buildings around the United Kingdom when Queen Elizabeth II's passing was announced. (MOD Crown Copyright)

Crowds gathered around royal palaces in London to show their respects within minutes of Queen Elizabeth II's passing being announced. (MOD Crown Copyright)

of Buckingham Palace. It simply stated that "The Queen died peacefully at Balmoral this afternoon." And recorded that The King and Queen Consort would return to London the following day. Large crowds began to gather outside Buckingham Palace and other royal residences to express their condolences. Floral tributes started to be laid at the gates. And, in a sign of the times, world leaders, celebrities and ordinary people began posting their own tributes online.

The first statement in the name of the new King was issued by Buckingham Palace on its website and social media feeds, expressing his sadness at his beloved mother's death. "We mourn profoundly the passing of a cherished sovereign and a much-loved mother. I know her loss will be deeply felt throughout the country, the Realms, and the Commonwealth, and by countless people around the world," said The King. "During this period of mourning and change, my family and I will be comforted and sustained by our knowledge of the respect and deep affection in which The Queen was so widely held."

The Prime Minister Liz Truss appeared at a lectern in Downing Street to pay tribute to the late monarch, saying: "Queen Elizabeth II was the rock on which modern Britain was built." Truss concluded her tribute by declaring, "God save the King", for the first time. This was the first public evidence of the transition from Queen to King had taken place. From now on The King's government would be conducting The King's business. ●

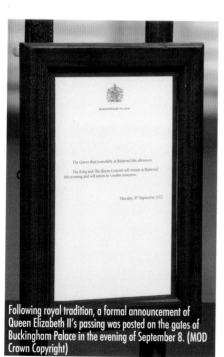

Following royal tradition, a formal announcement of Queen Elizabeth II's passing was posted on the gates of Buckingham Palace in the evening of September 8. (MOD Crown Copyright)

Following the announcement of The Queen's passing on the evening of September 8, 2022, Buckingham Palace was soon surrounded by huge crowds. (MOD Crown Copyright)

THE KING'S FIRST MESSAGE

September 9, 2022

Across Britain and the Commonwealth, a period of official mourning for Queen Elizabeth II got underway. Flags were at half mast, church services were held, and military units fired gun salutes. Crowds continued to gather outside royal residences to lay floral tributes and, increasingly, toy Paddington Bears started to appear in tribute to the late Queen's famous Platinum Jubilee television appearance with the character.

After spending the night at Balmoral Castle,

King Charles III returned to London later on September 9 to carry out his new royal duties. In a major break from tradition, he stopped his Rolls-Royce outside the gates of Buckingham Palace and strode over to meet the crowds of people gathered to show their respects. Accompanied by his wife, The King spoke to the crowds, viewed the tributes to his mother and then symbolically walked through the palace gates to begin his work as monarch. These historic events were broadcast live on rolling news channels and would set the tone for the coming days as The King appeared determined

to get out and meet the crowds of well-wishers who gathered wherever he went.

Once inside the palace he recorded his first royal video address in the Blue Drawing Room, which was released to the media later in the day and posted on the royal family's social media feeds.

In it, The King paid tribute to his late mother, saying: "'I speak to you today with feelings of profound sorrow. Throughout her life, Her Majesty The Queen - my beloved mother - was an inspiration and example to me and to all my family, and we owe her the most heartfelt debt

King Charles III returned to London on September 9 and before entering Buckingham Palace he stepped out of his official car to greet the crowds gathered at its gates. (MOD Crown Copyright)

The new King and his wife inspect tributes outside the gates of Buckingham Palace. Over the coming days the tributes kept coming and soon had to be moved to nearby royal parks. (MOD Crown Copyright)

The new King's first official events after returning to London were to meet Prime Minister Liz Truss to ensure continuity of state business. @RoyalFamily)

Camilla, Queen Consort accompanied her husband as he talked to the crowds outside Buckingham Palace. (MOD Crown Copyright)

any family can owe to their mother; for her love, affection, guidance, understanding and example. I pay tribute to my mother's memory and I honour her life of service. I know that her death brings great sadness to so many of you and I share that sense of loss beyond measure with you all."

Then he followed his mother's example and pledged his duty to a life of service. "I too now solemnly pledge myself throughout the remaining time God grants me, to uphold the constitutional principles at the heart of our nation. Wherever you may live in the United Kingdom or in the realms and territories across the world and whatever maybe your background and beliefs I shall endeavour to serve you with loyalty, respect and love, as I have throughout my life."

For the first time, he revealed details of the changes to the titles and duties of the royal family members. His wife was to take on the role of Queen Consort and his eldest son and his wife would be known as the Duke and Duchess of Cornwall. His son William would also be the new Prince of Wales.

He closed the speech, saying: "And to my darling Mama, as you begin your last great journey to join my dear late Papa, I want simply to say this: thank you. Thank you for your love and devotion to our family and to the family of nations you have served so diligently all these years. May 'flights of Angels sing thee to thy rest.'" ●

ACCESSION DAY FOR THE NEW KING

September 10, 2022

King Charles III signs his oath to uphold the position of the Church in Scotland, during the Accession Council meeting at James's Palace as part of the historic ceremony to proclaim him as Britain's new monarch. (Photo by Victoria Jones / POOL / AFP/Getty Images)

Although King Charles III automatically became monarch the moment his mother passed, many of the legal mechanisms for establishing his reign did not immediately take place. Constitutional and legal niceties dictate that senior members of the royal family, government ministers and church leaders gather to enact key measures of the transfer of royal power.

For centuries these ancient traditions took place behind closed doors but for King Charles III's accession, they took place in public for the first time when the Accession Council met on September 10 in the State Apartments of St James's Palace. This was a key part of the Operation London Bridge plan, and it is believed King Charles III was instrumental in pushing for it to be broadcast live for the first time as part of his drive to make his reign as open and transparent as possible.

The Accession Council is made up of the Privy Council – a 700 strong group of senior serving and retired government ministers, other politicians, the Lord Mayor and aldermen of the City of London and Commonwealth high commissioners. There was not enough room in St James's Palace for all 700 of the council so only 177 were invited, the majority after being selected by ballot. The group included all living former Prime Ministers and leaders of major political parties, with the exception of the

> ## "For centuries these ancient traditions took place behind closed doors but for King Charles III's accession, they took place in public for the first time"

former Labour Party leader Jeremy Corbyn, who chose not to attend.

For the first time, the clerk of the Privy Council, Richard Tilbrook, read aloud the Accession Proclamation, saying:

"Whereas it has pleased Almighty God to call to His Mercy our late Sovereign Lady Queen Elizabeth the Second of Blessed and Glorious Memory, by whose Decease the Crown of the United Kingdom of Great Britain and Northern

Ireland is solely and rightfully come to The Prince Charles Philip Arthur George. We, therefore, the Lords Spiritual and Temporal of this Realm and Members of the House of Commons, together with other members of Her late Majesty's Privy Council and representatives of the Realms and Territories, Aldermen and Citizens of London, and others, do now hereby with one voice and Consent of Tongue and Heart publish and proclaim that The Prince Charles Philip Arthur George is now, by the Death of our late Sovereign ➲

Coldstream Guardsmen cheer the new King after the proclamation ceremony at St James's Palace. (MOD Crown Copyright)

of Happy Memory, become our only lawful and rightful Liege Lord Charles the Third, by the Grace of God of the United Kingdom of Great Britain and Northern Ireland and of His other Realms and Territories, King, Head of the Commonwealth, Defender of the Faith, to whom we do acknowledge all Faith and Obedience with humble Affection; beseeching God by whom Kings and Queens do reign to bless His Majesty with long and happy Years to reign over us.

"Given at St James's Palace this tenth day of September in the year of Our Lord wo thousand and twenty-two.

"God Save the King."

Those present were then invited to the platform to sign the proclamation before the arrival of the new King. He told the council: "I know how deeply you, the entire nation – and I think I may say the whole world – sympathise with me in the irreparable loss we have all suffered. It is the greatest consolation to me to know of the sympathy expressed by so many to my sisters and brothers and that such overwhelming affection and support should be extended to our whole family in our loss."

He promised to follow in the example of

> **"In a mark of loyalty to the new King, flags flew at full-mast at 11am as the proclamation was being read, before being returned to half-mast until the day of the late Queen's funeral."**

The Friary Court was full of members of the public who had gathered at St James's Palace to hear - and record on their mobile phones - the new King proclaimed. (MOD Crown Copyright)

his late mother, saying: "I know that I shall be upheld by the affection and loyalty of the peoples whose sovereign I have been called upon to be, and that in the discharge of these duties I will be guided by the counsel of their elected parliaments. In all this, I am profoundly encouraged by the constant support of my beloved wife. I take this opportunity to confirm my willingness and intention to continue the tradition of surrendering the hereditary revenues, including the Crown Estate, to my government for the benefit of all, in return for the Sovereign Grant, which supports my official duties as Head of State and Head of Nation. And in carrying out the heavy task that has been laid upon me, and to which I now dedicate what remains to me of my life, I pray for the guidance and help of Almighty God."

Under the terms of the 1707 Anglo-Scottish Union, The King was then required to take and subscribe the oath relating to the 'security' of the Church of Scotland. The King faithfully promised and swore that he would maintain and

preserve the settlement of the true Protestant religion as established by the laws made in Scotland, as well as upholding the rights and privileges of the Church of Scotland. The King then signed two identical documents recording the taking of the oath. This was witnessed by the Queen Consort, the new Prince of Wales, the Lord Chancellor, the Secretary of State for Scotland, the First Minister of Scotland, the Lord Advocate, the Advocate General for Scotland and the Lord President of the Court of Session.

During the Accession Council, The King signed several documents, known as orders in council, setting out how state business would be conducted in Britain and around the

An hour after the initial reading the new King was proclaimed from the steps of the Royal Exchange in the City of London. Proclamation events continued across the country in the following days. (MOD Crown Copyright)

Commonwealth. These included the formal designation of the day of Queen Elizabeth's state funeral as a bank holiday. For the first time, these included requirements set by the 2011 Sovereign Grant Act to regulate the funding of the royal family and its property. The dry business of state was briefly interrupted when The King had to re-arrange the ink pots and pens as he signed the parchment documents.

Once the formal business of the Accession Council was concluded, the focus moved outside to the Proclamation Gallery of Friary Court in St James's Palace, where a crowd had gathered to hear David White, the Garter King of Arms re-read the Accession Proclamation at 11am. State trumpeters from the Household Cavalry performed, and then Guardsmen of the Coldstream Guards removed their bearskins to give three cheers for their new King, for the first time.

In a mark of loyalty to the new King, flags flew at full-mast at 11am as the proclamation was being read, before being returned to half-mast until the day of the late Queen's funeral.

According to ancient tradition, the Accession Proclamation was now to be read out in cities, towns and villages across Britain, as well as around the Commonwealth. This was a throwback to the days before newspapers or

Princes William and Harry, along with their wives, met well-wishers outside Windsor Castle in a show of family unity. (@RoyalFamily)

other forms of modern media when important government announcements were read out in market squares and other public places for the ordinary people to hear.

This tradition was continued in a bid to involve the wider public directly in the King's accession in their own communities and hundreds of similar events took place over the next two or three days.

The first of these Accession Proclamations took place from the steps of the Royal Exchange in the City of London, within an hour of the ceremony in St James's Palace. Timothy Duke, Clarenceux King of Arms, flanked by heralds the Lord Mayor and other city office holders re-read the proclamation as hundreds of people looked on.

Back at Buckingham Palace, The King was continuing with the business of state, holding audiences with the Prime Minister, senior cabinet ministers, leaders of opposition parties, the Archbishop of Canterbury and The Dean of Westminster. ●

On the balcony of St James's Palace, David White –the Garter King of Arms - read the proclamation of the new King in public for the first time. (MOD Crown Copyright)

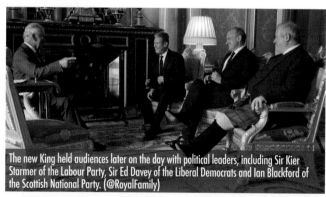

The new King held audiences later on the day with political leaders, including Sir Kier Starmer of the Labour Party, Sir Ed Davey of the Liberal Democrats and Ian Blackford of the Scottish National Party. (@RoyalFamily)

Members of Queen Elizabeth II's family walked out of the gates of the Balmoral Estate to view the many floral tributes left by sympathisers. (@RoyalFamily)

Eight state trumpeters of the Household Cavalry Mounted Regiment were on hand to perform during the proclamation of the new King. (MOD Crown Copyright)

Queen Elizabeth II left Balmoral on the morning of September 11 to head to Edinburgh to lie in state. (@ RoyalFamily)

THE KING IS PROCLAIMED

September 11, 2022

The lines of ponies and tractors arrayed in Scottish fields in tribute as Queen Elizabeth II's hearse passed caught the mood of the country.

After leaving Balmoral Castle early on the morning of Sunday September, 11 the hearse followed by vehicles carrying the Princess Royal, accompanied by her husband, Vice Admiral Sir Tim Laurence, passed through the small town of Ballatar before heading to Aberdeen, Dundee, and Edinburgh. The coffin bearing Queen Elizabeth II was draped with the Scottish version of the Royal Standard, symbolising her connection to Scotland and the unique constitutional position of Scotland in the United Kingdom. The late Queen's ancestors ruled Scotland long before the creation of Great Britain by the 1707 Act of Union.

Helicopters hired by news organisations followed the royal funeral convoy as it travelled south to the Scottish capital. Their live footage captured the scenes as people lined the route to show their respects. The massing of tractors by Aberdeenshire farmers and the lines of ponies in fields were graphic demonstrations of the affection felt by ordinary people for the late monarch. This was the first sign that the public wanted to be engaged on an unprecedented scale

By the afternoon the royal funeral cortège had passed over the Forth Crossing and was heading towards the Scottish capital. @RoyalFamily)

in the unfolding historic events.

As the convoy carrying Queen Elizabeth II headed to Edinburgh, events were taking place across the United Kingdom and the Commonwealth to proclaim her eldest son, King Charles III. Three 'national' proclamations took place at 12 noon, one in each of Edinburgh, Cardiff, and Belfast.

The King's Body Guard for Scotland (The Royal Company of Archers) and the Guard of Honour marched from Edinburgh Castle Esplanade to the city's Mercat Cross where Lord Lyon King of Arms, Joseph Morrow, made the first proclamation "to the people of Edinburgh." This was followed by a 21-gun salute from Edinburgh Castle, at which the proclamation was made a second time, on the Castle Drawbridge at 12.30pm "to the people of Scotland."

In Cardiff, a Proclamation Guard made up of 26 soldiers of the 3rd Battalion, The Royal Welsh Regiment, supported by the Band of the Royal Welsh and accompanied by the

The Royal Gibraltar Regiment prepare to fire a gun salute after the proclamation of The King on 'The Rock'. (MOD Crown Copyright)

Thousands of people lined Edinburgh's historic Royal Mile to view the arrival of Queen Elizabeth II. (MOD Crown Copyright)

Lord Lyon King of Arms, Joseph Morrow, made the first proclamation "to the people of Edinburgh" at the city's Mercat Cross. This was followed by a 21-gun salute from Edinburgh Castle. (MOD Crown Copyright)

The new King is proclaimed on the steps of Lancaster Town Hall. Hundreds of similar ceremonies took place across Britain and the Commonwealth. (Tim Ripley)

regimental mascot - Shenkin the goat - marched from City Hall along Boulevard de Nantes, North Road, and Duke Street to Cardiff Castle. The Lord Lieutenant for South Glamorgan, Morfudd Meredith, and Wales Herald of Arms Extraordinary, Thomas Lloyd, made the "Proclamation for Wales," in Welsh and English at 12:00. They did so from a dais in the grounds of Cardiff Castle. And, after a 21-gun salute, the audience sang God Save the King and Hen Wlad Fy Nhadau (Land of my fathers).

In Belfast, Norroy and Ulster King of Arms, Robert Noel, made the Northern Ireland Proclamation at the State Entrance to Hillsborough Castle, in the presence of representatives of civil and military establishments in the province. In attendance were the secretary of state for Northern Ireland, the minister of state for Northern Ireland, Democratic Unionist Party leader Sir Jeffrey Donaldson and Alliance leader Naomi Long. Sinn Féin representatives did not attend.

This was just the start and according to

tradition, the Accession Proclamation was also read out in suitable locations around England and Wales by high sheriffs, lord mayors, mayors, and others civic leaders. In Scotland, sheriffs, lord provosts and provosts officiated. Lord mayors and mayors in Northern Ireland conducted the ceremonies. These attracted audiences of several hundred people in front of town halls or other civic buildings. There was

> **"Helicopters hired by news organisations followed the royal funeral convoy as it travelled south to the Scottish capital."**

added poignancy when the participants sang God Save the King for the first time.

The span of the new King's domain was made apparent as the Accession Proclamation was read during the day across the Commonwealth in overseas British territories, Crown Dependencies, and countries where the British monarch is the head of state. This ranged from the States of Guernsey and Alderney to Australian Parliament House in Canberra. Each had its own distinctive character, including the one read out in Maori in the New Zealand parliament.

Back in Scotland, the final stages of Queen Elizabeth's 175 mile-long journey to Edinburgh was underway. As the royal convoy passed over the Forth Crossing and approached the Scottish capital the crowds got bigger and when it entered Edinburgh's historic Royal Mile the narrow streets were tightly packed. After passing down the Royal Mile and arriving at the Palace of Holyroodhouse, the late Queen's Coffin was placed at rest in the Throne Room overnight. ●

THE DAY OF TWO

September 12, 2022

Monday, September 12, 2022 was the 'day of two parliaments' for King Charles III as he continued his round of events, dubbed Operation Spring Tide, to mark his accession in the nations of the United Kingdom.

The morning saw The King, and his wife attend Westminster Hall to receive addresses from both houses of the United Kingdom Parliament. The ancient building, which dates from 1097, has been the venue for many historic events, including the trials of Guy Fawkes of gunpowder and treason plot fame and King Charles I at the end of the English Civil War.

After hearing the best wishes from the lords and elected members of the UK parliament, King Charles III headed for the Scottish capital, Edinburgh, for the next phase of his accession and to lead the lying-at-rest of his mother in St Giles Cathedral.

The events in Edinburgh were unprecedented in the history of the British royal family. Queen Elizabeth II was the first monarch to die in Scotland since James V of Scotland in 1542. Since George VI's death in 1952, the constitutional position of Scotland has been transformed with the establishment of the Scottish Parliament in 1999. The 1707 Act of

> "The King said: "My mother felt, as I do, the greatest admiration for the Scottish people, for their magnificent achievements and their indomitable spirit"

PARLIAMENTS

The King and Queen Consort in Westminster Hall. (UK Parliament)

King Charles III invested the Guard of Honour from the Royal Regiment of Scotland before his mother was moved to lie in state in St Giles Cathedral. (MOD Crown Copyright)

The new King stood vigil over his mother in St Giles Cathedral, alongside the Royal Company of Archers. (@RoyalFamily)

Thousands of mourners filed passed Queen Elizabeth II as she lay in state in the Scottish capital. (MOD Crown Copyright)

Union saw the old Scottish Parliament dissolved and elected representatives take their seats in the London parliament.

Queen Elizabeth II had opened the new Scottish Parliament in 1999 and her eldest son followed in her footsteps by accepting an invitation to receive the condolences of the devolved institution on September 12.

After arriving in Edinburgh, he first had to lead the mourning for his mother in the Scottish capital. In a day steeped in ceremony, at the Palace of Holyroodhouse, the lord provost first surrendered to The King the keys of the city [of Edinburgh], which the monarch then returned to him. Then The King, joined by his two brothers and sister, accompanied by her husband Vice Admiral Sir Tim Laurence, walked in procession behind the late Queen's coffin as it was moved by hearse to St Giles' Cathedral. Guns were fired every minute from Edinburgh Castle as the Procession traversed the Royal Mile. The last round fired as the hearse stopped outside the cathedral.

The bearer party from the Royal Regiment of Scotland, accompanied by an escort from the Royal Company of Archers, carried the coffin into the cathedral and the Crown of Scotland was placed on it. The Crown of Scotland was made in its present form for King James V of Scotland and forms part of the 'Honours of Scotland'.

A service of thanksgiving was then held to celebrate the late Queen's life and highlight her association with Scotland, led by the minister of St Giles' Cathedral. The King and The Queen Consort later drove to the Scottish Parliament, where the session opened with two minutes' silence. The only business was consideration of a Motion of Condolence moved by the first minister.

Responding to the motion, The King said:

"My mother felt, as I do, the greatest admiration for the Scottish people, for their magnificent achievements and their indomitable spirit, and it was the greatest comfort for her to know, in turn, the true affection in which she was held. The knowledge of that deep and abiding bond must be, to us, a solace as we mourn the end of a life of incomparable service."

He told the Scottish Parliament that the title of Duke of Rothesay and his other Scottish titles would now pass to his elder son, William.

"I take up my new duties with thankfulness for all that Scotland has given me, with resolve to seek always the welfare of our country and its people, and with whole-hearted trust in your good will and good counsel as we take forward that task together," said The King.

The Queen's coffin remained at the Cathedral for 24 hours, guarded by the Royal Company of Archers, which allowed around 33,000 people to file past and pay their respects. In the evening The King, Prince Andrew, Prince Edward, and the Princess Royal held a vigil at the cathedral, a custom known as the Vigil of the Princes. Princess Anne was the first woman to participate in the historic tradition. ●

The King and Queen Consort received a warm welcome from crowds at Hillsborough Castle. (MOD Crown Copyright)

THE KING IN NORTHERN IRELAND

September 13, 2022

After a day spent journeying between London and Edinburgh, The King and Queen Consort travelled to Northern Ireland on the next leg of Operation Spring Tide.

Northern Ireland's history of community division and conflict had been a source of much concern to Queen Elizabeth II who had made great efforts to bridge divisions on the island of Ireland. The late Queen's historic visit to the Irish Republic in 2011 had been hailed as a milestone, and a year later she travelled to Belfast and shook hands with former IRA commander Martin McGuinness. The symbolism was enormous as McGuinness had played a leading role in the IRA when it had blown up and killed her husband's uncle, Lord Louis Mountbatten in 1979.

The transformation of Northern Ireland since the 1998 Good Friday peace agreement was on show during The King's visit but its precarious political situation was also evident.

After landing at Belfast City Airport, the royal party headed for Hillsborough Castle, The King's official residence in Northern Ireland. The King and his wife undertook a short walkabout

outside the castle before moving inside and viewing an exhibition of pictures showing the late Queen's visits to the region during her reign. The King then received a message of condolence from the Northern Ireland Assembly. In an unscripted moment, The King was involved in an altercation with a malfunctioning pen that sprung a leak. Videos of the incident went viral

Well-wishers travelled to Hillsborough Castle to lay tributes to Queen Elizabeth II and to meet King Charles III as he made his first visit to Northern Ireland. (MOD Crown Copyright)

on social media.

Unlike in Scotland and Wales, the devolved assembly in Northern Ireland was not up and running because of a dispute over the trade protocol with the European Union. So, in the absence of a first minister, it fell to the Speaker of the Northern Ireland Assembly, Alex Maskey, to present the message of condolence to The King. Maskey is a lifelong Irish Republican who had been imprisoned without trial by British troops in the early 1970s. He was elected in 2002 as the first Sinn Fein lord mayor of Belfast, where he famously adorned his office with both the Union Flag and the Irish Tricolour.

Maskey praised the late Queen, whom he said had not been a "distant observer" but a participant in efforts to build peace in Ireland. He said Queen Elizabeth II had "demonstrated how individual acts of positive leadership can help break down barriers and encourage reconciliation. She showed that a small and insignificant gesture – a visit, a handshake, crossing the street or speaking a few words of Irish – can make a huge difference in changing attitudes and building relationships."

Responding, The King said: "It is fitting that we should meet at Hillsborough, which my mother knew so well, and in whose beautiful rose garden she always took such pleasure. In the years since she began her long life of public service, my mother saw Northern Ireland pass through momentous and historic changes. Through all those years, she never ceased to pray for the best of times for this place and for its people, whose stories she knew, whose sorrows our family had felt, and for whom she had a great affection and regard. My mother felt deeply, I know, the significance of the role she herself played in bringing together those whom history had separated, and in extending a hand to make possible the healing of long-held hurts."

The King and Queen Consort subsequently gave a reception at Hillsborough Castle for elected representatives before the royal couple attended a Service of Reflection celebrating the late Queen's life at St. Anne's Cathedral in Belfast.

Back in Edinburgh, the laying-in-state of Queen Elizabeth II came to an end and her coffin was taken by hearse to Edinburgh Airport where a Royal Air Force C-17 Globemaster was waiting to fly it to RAF Northolt, in west London. A Royal Air Force Regiment bearer party carried the coffin onto the aircraft, past a guard of honour from the Royal Regiment of Scotland. The Princess Royal and her husband, Vice Admiral Sir Timothy Laurence, boarded the aircraft for the flight. During the journey the Scottish version of the Royal Standard that draped the coffin was replaced by the Royal Standard that is used in the remainder of the United Kingdom.

After landing, the late Queen's coffin was then driven in the State Hearse to Buckingham Palace along roads lined with thousands of people who stood in the rain to pay their respects. ●

> ## "It is fitting that we should meet at Hillsborough, which my mother knew so well, and in whose beautiful rose garden she always took such pleasure."

The corgi lovers of Northern Ireland turned out at Hillsborough Castle to show their respects to the new King. (MOD Crown Copyright)

Queen Elizabeth II arrives back at Buckingham Palace after driving from RAF Northolt along roads lined with people showing their respects. (MOD Crown Copyright)

An RAF C-17 Globemaster flew Queen Elizabeth II from Edinburgh Airport to RAF Northolt, using the official royal callsign, Kittyhawk, for the final time. (MOD Crown Copyright)

A bearer party of the RAF Regiment carried Queen Elizabeth II off a RAF C-17 Globemaster at RAF Northolt. (MOD Crown Copyright)

WESTMINSTER

September 14, 2022

Queen Elizabeth II left Buckingham Palace in a funeral procession to Westminster Hall, where she was to lie-in-state for five days. (MOD Crown Copyright)

With the return of Queen Elizabeth II to Buckingham Palace the night before, the focus of royal events switched to London. Preparations had been underway since the late Queen's passing to get the city ready for several days of high profile ceremonial events, as well as putting in place the necessary logistics and security arrangements for the arrival of hundreds of thousands of visitors. Streets were closed to traffic, railway stations prepared for additional passengers, international media organisations descended on London and police leave was cancelled to ensure maximum numbers of security personnel were available.

The preparations caused considerable disruption across London, but public reaction was almost universally positive. Planned industrial action by railway staff was even postponed until after the state funeral.

The first set piece event to show the nation's respect to Queen Elizabeth II was the movement of her coffin from Buckingham Palace to Westminster Hall, where it would lay in state until her funeral.

At 2.22pm on Wednesday, September 14 the Queen's Coffin was borne in-state from Buckingham Palace on a gun carriage of The King's Troop, Royal Horse Artillery, flanked by the escort party drawn from 1st Battalion, The Grenadier Guards, to the Palace of Westminster.

> **"It was a hugely solemn occasion and the centre of London fell largely silent as the gun carriage passed."**

HALL

The King and senior members of the royal family followed on behind the gun carriage carrying Queen Elizabeth II. (MOD Crown Copyright)

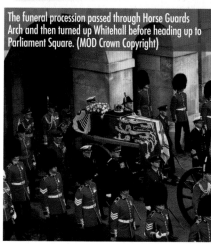

The funeral procession passed through Horse Guards Arch and then turned up Whitehall before heading up to Parliament Square. (MOD Crown Copyright)

A continuous vigil was kept over Queen Elizabeth II during her stay in Westminster Hall by the Body Guard of the Honourable Corps of Gentlemen at Arms, assisted at times by The King's Body Guard for Scotland (The Royal Company of Archers), The King's Body Guard of the Yeomen of the Guard, assisted by The Body of Yeomen Warders of Tower of London, and by soldiers of the Household Division. (MOD Crown Copyright)

In Hyde Park, 38 rounds were fired in a royal gun salute to mark each minute of the procession. 'Big Ben', the bell of the Great Clock of Westminster tolled 38 times.

The coffin was followed on foot by The King, the Prince of Wales, the Duke of Sussex, the Duke of York, the Earl of Wessex, the Princess Royal, Peter Phillips, the Duke of Gloucester, the Earl of Snowdon, and Vice Admiral Sir Tim Laurence. Other members of the royal family travelled separately.

Thousands of people lined the route as the royal party followed behind the gun carriage as it travelled down the Mall, across Horse Guards, and then on to Whitehall. It was a hugely

solemn occasion and the centre of London fell largely silent as the gun carriage passed.

After the coffin arrived The King and Queen Consort, as well as other members of the royal family, attended a service for the reception conducted by the Archbishop of Canterbury and the Dean of Westminster. This, like the Accession Council, was televised for the first time. A limited number of nominated members of parliament and peers also attended, as did members of the devolved assemblies in Northern Ireland, Scotland and Wales, and Commonwealth high commissioners.

The Body Guard of the Honourable Corps of Gentlemen at Arms and The King's Body Guard of the Yeomen of the Guard stood guard around the late Queen in the historic setting of Westminster Hall. The coffin was draped with the Royal Standard on which lay the 'Instruments of State': the Imperial State Crown, Orb and Sceptre.

Once the formal ceremonial event was completed work began to open Westminster Hall for members of the public to pay their respect. Thousands of people had already began

queuing across Lambert Brigade and along the South Bank of the Thames.

Just after 5pm, the first members of the public were allowed into Westminster Hall. Throughout the night and coming days, more and more joined the queue until stretched down to Southwark Park. At its peak, wait time in the queue was more than 22 hours.

Volunteer organisations were mobilised to provide hot food and drinks for the people in the queue as they waited through the cold nights. The queue remained good natured, and spirits stayed high among those aiming to show their respects to the late Queen. Once inside the ancient building, the queue divided to pass on either side of the catafalque displaying Queen Elizabeth II's coffin. The public were allowed a brief moment to stand and view the coffin before heading to the exit. Although brief, few who experienced the Lying-in-State said they would forget their time in Westminster Hall.

In a new twist to an ancient tradition, the whole of the Lying-in-State was streamed live over the internet. ●

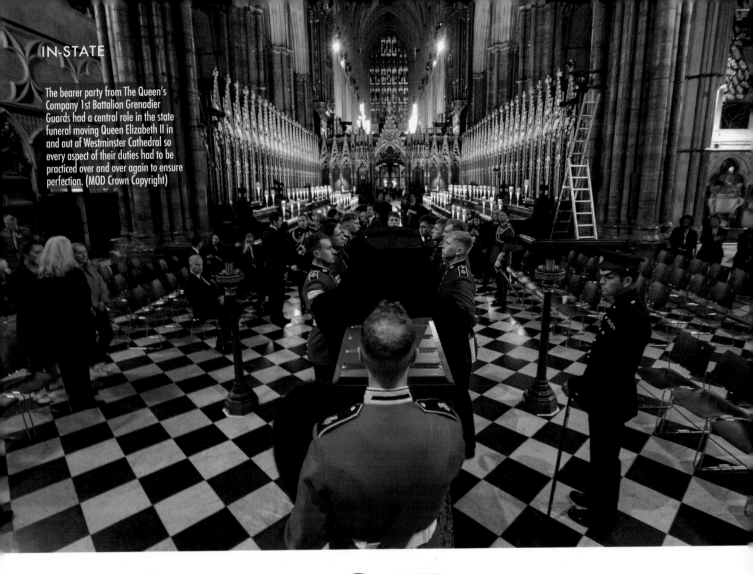

The bearer party from The Queen's Company 1st Battalion Grenadier Guards had a central role in the state funeral moving Queen Elizabeth II in and out of Westminster Cathedral so every aspect of their duties had to be practiced over and over again to ensure perfection. (MOD Crown Copyright)

A DAY OF ROYAL VISITS

September 15, 2022

On Thursday, September 15 the tempo of royal events dropped with The King and Queen Consort spending the day at their private residences, Highgrove House in Gloucestershire and Ray Mill House in Wiltshire, respectively. State business, however, continued with The King speaking on the telephone with several world leaders, including the presidents of Rwanda, Greece, Germany and The King of Saudi Arabia.

Other members of the royal family travelled around Britain to visit memorials to Queen Elizabeth II, attend civic events and meet members of the public. The Princess Royal visited Glasgow and spent some time at a reception with representatives from various organisations of which the late Queen served as patron, including Friends of Glasgow Cathedral, Glasgow Caledonian University, the Royal

British Legion of Scotland, YMCA, the Royal Scottish Society of Arts, the Royal Scottish Country Dance Society, Lambhill Stables, and the RSNO.

The Prince and Princess of Wales view floral tributes to Queen Elizabeth II outside Sandringham House in Norfolk. (@RoyalFamily)

Prince William and his wife took time to look at floral tributes outside Sandringham House in Norfolk and meet members of the public.

This was the first full day of The Queen's Lying-in-State and the public queue continued to grow. At 5am, the queue was 2.1 miles long stretching as far as Southwark Bridge. Those waiting in line were given a coloured wristband to prevent queue jumping and to allow for food and comfort breaks.

Defence Secretary Ben Wallace and Scottish Secretary Alister Jack, both members of the Royal Company of Archers, took part in the vigil around Queen Elizabeth II's coffin.

Behind the scenes preparations were well underway for Queen Elizabeth II's state funeral, which was now only four days away. In the darkness before dawn, the military personnel who were to play a central role in the funeral carried out a full rehearsal as the capital slept. Thousands of soldiers, sailors and airmen from

Every drill manoeuvre was practiced repeatedly during the rehearsal to make sure it went off perfectly during the state funeral. (MOD Crown Copyright)

Britain and the Commonwealth donned their full ceremonial uniforms and recreated every aspect of the funeral to make sure it would go like clockwork on the day. Every aspect was practiced, even down to carrying a replica coffin into Westminster Abbey.

The proceedings were overseen by Major General Christopher John Ghika, the general commanding officer of London District, and his garrison sergeant major, Warrant Officer 1 Vern Stokes, to make sure everyone was up to scratch. As dawn was breaking, the two veterans of royal ceremonial events declared themselves happy

> ## "This was the first full day of The Queen's Lying-in-State and the public queue continued to grow. At 5am, the queue was 2.1 miles long"

that their troops were ready for the highest profile event for the British armed forces in recent times.

At the same time as General Ghika and GSM Stokes were fine tuning the plans for the parade, the Commissioner of the Metropolitan Police, Sir Mark Peter Rowley, and his officers practiced setting and running the biggest security operation London has ever seen. With US President Joe Biden and hundreds of other world leaders and VIPs attending, this would represent a security task like no other. ●

Members of the public filed past Queen Elizabeth II's coffin around the clock during her lying-in-state in Westminster Hall. (MOD Crown Copyright)

Thousands of service personnel practiced their part in the state funeral in a full dress rehearsal held during the early hours of September 15. (MOD Crown Copyright)

THE KING IN WALES

September 16, 2022

The final phase of Operation Spring Tide took place on Friday September 16, when The King and Queen Consort visited Cardiff to hear the condolences of the Senedd, the Welsh Parliament.

The visit coincided with Owain Glyndŵr Day, which celebrated the last native-born Prince of Wales who famously led a revolt against English rule. King Charles III had held the title since 1958 and was invested in a high profile ceremony in 1969. His investiture at Caernarfon Castle had caused considerable controversy among Welsh nationalists and Welsh language

speakers. They protested that the granting of the title to a member of the British royal family was a colonial imposition. In 1969, two people had died when they were allegedly planting a bomb in protest the night before the investiture and thousands of people joined protest marches on the day.

The granting of the Prince of Wales title on Prince William after The King's accession to the throne drew similar controversy but it did not translate into any street demonstrations or protests during the royal visit on September 16.

The royal couple flew to Wales by helicopter and attended a service of prayer and reflection for the life of the late Queen at Cardiff's

> "Through all the years of her reign, the land of Wales could not have been closer to my mother's heart. Wales had a special place in her heart."

The Prince and Princess of Wales visited Commonwealth military contingents preparing to participate in the state funeral. (MOD Crown Copyright)

The King greets an old friend from the Welsh Guards on duty outside the Senedd. (MOD Crown Copyright)

The Senedd, or Welsh Parliament, in Cardiff offered its condolences to The King on September 16. (Senedd/Welsh Parliament)

And they kept coming... Day after day the queue to view Queen Elizabeth II got bigger. (Katie Chan)

Llandaff Cathedral. Then, after travelling to the Senedd building in Cardiff Bay, the Welsh Parliament presented its motion of condolence to The King, who replied in both Welsh and English.

"Through all the years of her reign, the land of Wales could not have been closer to my mother's heart. Wales had a special place in her heart," he told the Senedd. "I know she took immense pride in your many great achievements – even as she also felt with you deeply in time of sorrow. It must surely be counted the greatest privilege to belong to a land that could inspire such devotion. I am resolved to honour that selfless example, in the spirit of the words by which I have always tried to live my own life.

"It was a privilege to be Prince of Wales for so long. Now my son, William, will bear the title. He has a deep love for Wales. I take up my new duties with immense gratitude for the privilege of having been able to serve as Prince of Wales. That ancient title, dating from the time of those great Welsh rulers, like Llywelyn ap Gruffudd, whose memory is still rightly honoured, I now pass to my son, William, whose love for this corner of the Earth is made all the greater by the years he himself has spent here.

"Like my beloved mother before me, I know we all share a love for this special land. Having visited the Senedd regularly since it was founded, and having heard your heartfelt words today, I know we all share the deepest commitment to the welfare of the people of this land and that we will all continue to work together to that end."

Afterwards in the formal session, The King and Queen Consort met members of the Welsh Youth Parliament and the elected members of the Senedd. They then went on a walkabout outside the Senedd building to meet well-wishers.

In the evening, the late Queen's children gathered in Westminster Hall to mount a vigil around their mother's coffin. The King, the Duke of York, the Earl of Wessex and the Princess Royal all stood guard in a modern version of the ancient tradition. ●

Queen Elizabeth II's children, led by The King, took their turn to stand vigil over their mother. (MOD Crown Copyright)

THE KING MEETS HIS PEOPLE

September 17, 2022

Three days into the opening of the public viewing of Queen Elizabeth II's coffin in Westminster Hall, the queue was just as long. And global news organisations had descended on London to report on the historic events in the build up to the late Queen's funeral.

The outpouring of public support for the royal family prompted The King and his eldest son, the Prince of Wales, to make made a surprise visit to the queue, just over the River Thames near Lambert Palace.

The King and the heir to the throne emerged from their armour-plated cars and surprised members of the public, some of whom had been waiting in the queue for more than 20 hours cheered and sang the national anthem as the royal walkabout got underway. The event was broadcast live after rolling news channels switched their coverage to show the two royals meeting the public. Police protection officers kept a close watch on the event, and one was heard telling the crowd to put their phones away and 'enjoy the moment'.

King Charles III shook hands with scores of people, thanking them for waiting upwards of 20-hours to view his mother lying-in-state. The King reportedly told one person waiting in the queue, "I hope you didn't get too frozen," after hearing about the freezing temperatures the previous night.

The King engaged with many in the crowd, who were keen to express their personal condolences. "Sorry for your loss," said one well-wisher to the new monarch.

Prince William received an equally warm welcome as he shook hands and greeted people, telling mourners who had waited overnight: "Thank you it means an awful lot."

The new Prince of Wales offered words of encouragement to those in the queue, telling one child: "You're over halfway," and commented to other well-wishers saying he was sorry they had had to wait for so long. They responded by telling Prince William that the wait was 'worth it'.

King Charles left around 20 minutes after arriving and was driven back to Buckingham Palace, but his son stayed longer to speak to more people. One woman in the queue told the Prince

> ## "Several people reportedly cried after meeting Prince William, with one woman telling him: "You'll be a brilliant king one day.""

she had been queuing for 13 hours already. He replied: "Thirteen hours? You're looking very good on 13 hours."

Prince William joked with one person in the queue that their trainers were a good choice of footwear for the queue. Several people reportedly cried after meeting Prince William, with one woman telling him: "You'll be a brilliant king one day."

After his walkabout, The King visited the Metropolitan Police's Special Operations Room

The King took time to meet police, military, and emergency service personnel co-ordinating operations in London during the laying-in-state. @RoyalFamily)

The King and the Prince of Wales made a surprise visit to the queue to thank mourners for their support. (@RoyalFamily)

Military chiefs took their turn to stand vigil over Queen Elizabeth in Westminster Hall. (MOD Crown Copyright)

in Lambeth to talk to many of the key personnel overseeing security operation across London. Deputy Assistant Commissioner Stuart Cundy told The King it was a 'hugely complex' operation surpassing the London 2012 Olympics, with up to 10,000 police officers on duty each day.

The King and Prince William were not the only royals out and about that day. Prince Edward and his wife, Sophie, Countess of Wessex, took time to speak to people outside Buckingham Palace.

During the evening, Queen Elizabeth II's eight grandchildren stood vigil over her coffin in Westminster Hall. Prince Harry was given permission by The King to wear military uniform for the ceremony.

Prince Harry stood at the foot of the coffin, with Prince William at the head. They were joined by their cousins Princesses Beatrice and Eugenie, Peter Phillips, Zara Tindall, Lady Louise Windsor and James, Viscount Severn.

Ahead of the vigil, Beatrice and Eugenie paid tribute to their 'dear Grannie', saying: "It has been the honour of our lives to have been your granddaughters and we're so very proud of you." ●

The King thanked the Chief of Defence Staff Admiral Tony Radakin for the efforts of the armed forces to prepare for the state funeral. (@RoyalFamily)

The head of the Royal Air Force, Air Chief Marshal Mike Wigston, was part of the honour guard of service chiefs during the vigil over Queen Elizabeth in Westminster Hall. (MOD Crown Copyright)

HEADS OF STATE

September 18, 2022

The King meets the prime minister of Antigua and Barbuda. (@Royal Family)

Sunday, September 18 was the last full day of Queen Elizabeth II's lying-in-state and, as the final hours approached before the historic event came to a close, the queue was closed and it began to shrink.

Those passing through Westminster Hall were joined during the day by many of the world leaders who were arriving in London ahead of the state funeral, including US President Joe Biden and French President Emmanuel Macron. They viewed the solemn scene from a VIP viewing platform high above Westminster Hall.

"To all the people of England, all the people in the United Kingdom, our hearts go out to you," Biden said after he signed a book of condolence and visited Queen Elizabeth II's lying-in-state. "You were fortunate to have had her for 70 years, we all were. The world's better for her."

Thousands of government officials, council staff, police officers and military personnel started to swing into action to make the final preparations for The Queen's funeral.

At 8pm, there was a national moment of reflection. Big Ben was supposed to strike twice, at the beginning and end of the minute's silence, but failed due to 'a minor technical issue'.

The silence was marked privately around Britain and the Commonwealth in people's homes with friends and family, out on doorsteps or in the street with neighbours, or at locally arranged community events and vigils.

The King issued a written message expressing his thanks to all the people who had participated in events since his mother's passing or sent messages of condolence.

"Over the last 10 days, my wife and I have been so deeply touched by the many messages of condolences and support we have received from this country and across the world," he said. "In London, Edinburgh, Hillsborough, and Cardiff we were moved beyond measure by everyone who took the trouble to come and pay their respects to the lifelong service of my dear mother, the late Queen. As we all prepare to say our last farewell, I wanted simply to take this opportunity to say thank you to all those countless people who have been such a support and comfort to my family and myself in this time of grief."

The final state duty of the day was to host a reception at Buckingham Palace for the hundreds of world leaders who had flown into London on the eve of the state funeral. ●

A Right Royal Guest List

Nearly 2,000 guests arrived in London on the evening before the state funeral of Queen Elizabeth II. In addition to 55 presidents and 25 prime ministers, the guest listed included 18 reigning monarchs from Europe, Africa, and Asia, as well as members of the Queen's extended family, friends, cabinet ministers, religious representatives, courtiers, and employees.

Other representatives included recipients of the Victoria and George Crosses, UK and devolved legislatures, the Church of England and representatives from charities linked to the late Queen. Almost 200 people who were recognised in The Queen's Birthday Honours earlier in 2022 also joined the congregation, including those who had made contributions to the response to the COVID-19 pandemic.

Foreign dignitaries - ministers, government officials and ambassadors – from more than 200 countries and Commonwealth territories attended. These included representatives from 168 countries, out of 193 United Nations member states, two UN observer states and Kosovo.

The presence of US President Joe Biden, the Emperor of Japan and almost every head of state or monarchy in Europe and the Commonwealth showed the high regard the late Queen was held in by her fellow world leaders. This even extended to these VIPs - except for President Biden - agreeing to travel on buses to Westminster Abbey.

Military personnel helped organise the queue for the laying-in-state, including checking the ID bands of mourners. (MOD Crown Copyright)

Military contingents from around the Commonwealth – in their distinctive uniforms – had a central role in the state funeral and rehearsed repeatedly in the days leading up to the event. (MOD Crown Copyright)

Tributes to Queen Elizabeth II kept coming and there were so many that royal household staff had to move many to displays in the royal parks around London. (@Royal Family)

A ROYAL FAREWELL
QUEEN ELIZABETH

September 19, 2022

The bearer party of The Queen's Company, 1st Battalion, The Grenadier Guards carried Queen Elizabeth II into Westminster Abbey. (MOD Crown Copyright)

II'S FUNERAL

Queen Elizabeth's lying-in-state came to an end at 6.30am on the morning of her funeral as the final members of the public were admitted to Westminster Hall. Digital Culture Media and Sport Secretary Michelle Donelan later revealed in a media interview that more than 250,000 people had paid their respects.

Many shops and businesses across the capital, including the London Stock Exchange, were shuttered as the day had been declared a bank holiday to allow staff to show their respects. Schools and other educational institutions were also closed. Hundreds of thousands of people started arriving in the capital early in the morning to watch the historic events. Some hardy individuals had camped out at key vantage points to secure a good view. In an unprecedented move, Heathrow Airport stopped all departures and arrivals for 30 minutes from 11.40am, to ensure silence over central London at key moments during the state funeral.

At 10.44am The Queen's coffin left Westminster Hall and headed towards Westminster Abbey carried on the State Gun Carriage pulled by 98 Royal Navy sailors. The King, members of the royal family and royal household followed in procession behind the carriage. It was something not seen since the state funeral of Sir Winston Churchill in 1965.

The tradition of sailors pulling the gun carriage dates from the 1901 state funeral of Queen Victoria, when the horses intended to pull her gun carriage became agitated and had to be replaced at short notice.

The procession – which was led by the massed pipes and drums of the Scottish and Irish Regiments, the Brigade of Gurkhas, and the Royal Air Force – included detachments from the armed forces of the Commonwealth, as well as detachments of the British armed forces who held a special relationship with Queen Elizabeth II.

The procession arrived at the West Gate ➲

At a family funeral service inside the King George VI Chapel, The King and his family gathered to say a final farewell to Queen Elizabeth II. (@Royal Family)

THE FUNERAL

of Westminster Abbey at 10.52am, where the bearer party lifted the coffin from the State Gun Carriage and carried it inside.

The Dean of Westminster conducted the service. British Prime Minister Liz Truss and Commonwealth Secretary-General Baroness Scotland read lessons. The Archbishop of York, the Cardinal Archbishop of Westminster, the Moderator of the General Assembly of the Church of Scotland, and the Free Churches Moderator all said prayers. The sermon was given by the Archbishop of Canterbury, who

also gave the commendation. The Dean of Westminster then pronounced the blessing.

Towards the end of the service, the Last Post was sounded followed by a two-minute's silence which was observed in the Abbey and throughout Britain. The National Anthem and a bagpipe lament (Sleep, dearie, sleep) brought the state funeral to a close at 12 noon. A wreath with flowers from Buckingham Palace, Highgrove and Clarence House had been placed on the coffin with a note from The King, "In loving and devoted memory. Charles R."

After the service, the coffin was borne through the Abbey and returned to the State Gun Carriage for the procession to Wellington Arch.

The King and members of the royal family again followed the late Queen's coffin in

procession, led by a mounted detachment of the Royal Canadian Mounted Police. Minute guns were fired in Hyde Park by The King's Troop and Royal Horse Artillery. The King's Guard gave a royal salute as the coffin passed the Queen Victoria Memorial outside Buckingham Palace. Big Ben tolled - its hammer muffled with leather - for the duration of the procession. The gun carriage, again pulled by sailors, reached Wellington Arch at Hyde Park Corner at around 1pm.

At Wellington Arch, the coffin was transferred to the State Hearse to travel to Windsor. As the hearse departed Wellington Arch at 1.37pm, the parade was given a royal salute and the National Anthem was played. The King and other members of the royal family then departed for

Thousands of mourners lined the Long Walk outside Windsor Castle to pay their respects to Queen Elizabeth II. (MOD Crown Copyright)

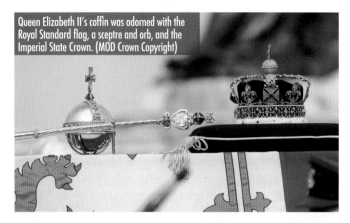

Queen Elizabeth II's coffin was adorned with the Royal Standard flag, a sceptre and orb, and the Imperial State Crown. (MOD Crown Copyright)

The final duty of The Queen's Company, 1st Battalion, The Grenadier Guards was to carry their late monarch into the King George VI Chapel. (MOD Crown Copyright)

After Queen Elizabeth II's funeral a ledger stone has been installed over her place of rest in the King George VI Chapel. (@Royal Family)

Westminster Abbey has been the venue for the funeral of British monarchs stretching back hundreds of years. (@Kensingston Palace)

"Prior to the final hymn, the Imperial State Crown, orb, and sceptre were removed from the coffin by the crown jeweller and placed on the altar by the Dean of Windsor."

Windsor by car.

When the coffin reached Windsor, the State Hearse slowed to join a procession to be formed up on Albert Road to travel via The Long Walk to St George's Chapel, for the Committal Service. Members of the royal family joined the procession in the quadrangle at Windsor Castle. Minute guns were fired on the East Lawn by The King's Troop and Royal Horse Artillery. The Sebastopol Bell and Curfew Tower Bell were tolled.

The procession halted at the bottom of the West Steps of St George's Chapel where a guard of honour, formed by the 1st Battalion, The Grenadier Guards, was mounted.

The Committal Service began 4pm. Alongside The King and members of the royal family,

the congregation comprised past and present members of the late Queen's household, including from her private estates. Also in attendance were Commonwealth governors-general and prime ministers. The Dean of Windsor conducted the service, with prayers said by the Rector of Sandringham, the Minister of Crathie Kirk and the Chaplain of Windsor Great Park. The choir of St George's Chapel sang during the service.

Prior to the final hymn, the Imperial State

Royal Navy sailors pulled the gun carriage carrying Queen Elizabeth II from Westminster Hall to Westminster Abbey. (MOD Crown Copyright)

Crown, orb, and sceptre were removed from the coffin by the crown jeweller and placed on the altar by the Dean of Windsor. At the end of the final hymn, The King placed The Queen's Company Camp Colour of the Grenadier Guards on the Coffin. At the same time, the lord chamberlain - the most senior officer of the royal household – 'broke', or unscrewed, his wand of office and placed it on the coffin.

As Queen Elizabeth II's coffin was lowered into the Royal Vault, the Dean of Windsor said a psalm and a commendation. Then the Garter King of Arms proclaimed the late Queen's styles and titles: "The late Most High, Most Mighty, and Most Excellent Monarch, Elizabeth the Second, by the Grace of God of the United Kingdom of Great Britain and Northern Ireland and of Her other Realms and Territories Queen, Head of the Commonwealth, Defender of the Faith, and Sovereign of the Most Noble Order of the Garter."

The sovereign's piper played a lament, and the Archbishop of Canterbury pronounced the blessing. The National Anthem concluded the service.

At 7.30pm, a private burial conducted by the Dean of Windsor took place in the King George VI Memorial Chapel. Queen Elizabeth II and her late husband were interred together, with her parents, King George VI and Queen Elizabeth, Queen Mother. A reinscribed ledger stone set into the floor included the names, birth, and death dates of all four, together with a metal star representing the Order of the Garter. ●

The ceremonial aspects of Queen Elizabeth II's state funeral went without a hitch (MOD/Crown Copyright)

12 HISTORIC DAYS

From Queen to King

For 12 days in September, 2022 history was made. Britain's longest reigning monarch passed away and a new King assumed his throne.

Although the plans for the accession of the new King and the funeral of Queen Elizabeth II had been laid many years before, there was still considerable uncertainty about what would happen when the Queen Elizabeth II passed away. How would people react? Would the huge ceremonial events run smoothly? How would the newly installed government of Prime Minister Liz Truss manage this constitutional transition?

The late Queen was 96 years old and was visibly getting frailer in the months up to her passing, so her family and the nation had readied themselves for the sad day. When news emerged on the morning of September 8 that Queen Elizabeth II was gravely ill, it was not a surprise.

In the desperately sad hours after his mothers passing, The King was understandably heavily involved in comforting his family. The return of the King to London on the following day set a very different tone. His impromptu walkabout outside Buckingham Palace on the evening of September 9 was covered live on television. His composure and empathy with the crowds won much praise. Later, his first ever royal television address had a huge audience in Britain and around the world. The King struck the right

chord, both paying tribute to his mother's life and re-assuring the public that he would try to follow her example.

The following day, the formal state business of The King's accession to the throne was broadcast live on television for the first time, showing that the new monarch wanted to open the work of the Crown to public view.

The proclamation of The King's accession from the balcony of St James's Palace saw the first formal public gathering where God Save the King rang out. Over the next two days similar events took place across Britain and the Commonwealth, allowing thousands of

Public affection for Queen Elizabeth II was shown in many ways. The royal residences around London and elsewhere were swamped by floral tributes. (MOD/Crown Copyright)

> ## "The King struck the right chord, both paying tribute to his mother's life and re-assuring the public that he would try to follow her example."

other people to join in singing the words for the first time.

Britain's constituent nations were placed at the heart of the accession celebrations and The King made visits over the next week to Edinburgh, Belfast and Cardiff to engage the devolved administrations, elected representatives and large crowds of ordinary people.

The lying-at-rest of Queen Elizabeth II overnight in Edinburgh's St Giles Cathedral meant that for two days the Scottish capital was the focus of world attention. A British monarch had not died in Scotland since 1542 and it symbolically highlighted the country's unique constitutional position in the United Kingdom. The King's engagement with the Scottish Parliament and government was in stark

On almost every day during the build up to his mother's funeral The King was out and about meeting people. (MOD/Crown Copyright)

contrast to comments made a few weeks earlier by the then UK Prime Minister Liz Truss that she would "ignore" the Scottish First Minister, Nicola Sturgeon.

The King's visit to Belfast the following day and his friendly engagement with political leaders from all communities, at a time of deep division in Northern Ireland also won praise.

Among the daily round of state and ceremonial events, The King went out of his way to meet ordinary people, often in unscripted and spontaneous walkabouts. His bodyguards must have been very nervous, but The King appeared to consider it important to meet his people. During the formal ceremonial events The King played his part to the full with good grace and composure, including on four occasions walking in procession behind his mother's coffin and twice standing in vigil. Few heads of state would have been allowed by their security teams to play such a public role. One observer suggested that no US President would ever have displayed such bravery.

King Charles III started his reign how he wants to continue - in the public eye and in close proximity with his people. ●

London was centre stage during Queen Elizabeth II's state funeral. (MOD/Crown Copyright)

For the first time as monarch, The King led the National Service of Remembrance at the Cenotaph in Whitehall. (MOD/Crown Copyright)

THE KING GETS TO WORK

First Months of the New Reign

After Liz Truss' fall The King asked Rishi Sunak to form his new government, the third one of 2022. (@RoyalFamily)

I n the days after Queen Elizabeth II's funeral the royal family quite understandably stood back from public view. However, the business of state continued, and Buckingham Palace posted on the royal family twitter feed on September 24 of The King working on his 'red boxes' of state papers.

In the last week of September 2022 members of the royal family restarted their programme of official visits. The new Prince and Princess of Wales made a trip to Wales to visit several charities at work, the Duke of Wessex travelled to German and Estonia to visit British troops on NATO duty and the Princess Royal visited military personnel who had been involved in the state funeral of her mother.

The new King and Queen Consort made their first joint public appearance on October 3 when then travelled to Dunfermline in Scotland to celebrate the district being granted city status. Dressed in a kilt, The King and his wife talked to well-wishers. In a reference to the famous pen incident at Hilsborough Castle, he was filmed at a formal signing ceremony handing the pen to his wife and adding with a laugh, "These things are so temperamental."

The royal calendar soon filled up with more events – it was business as usual for the royal family, as far as their public role was concerned. There were charities to support, military units to visit, civic buildings to open and foreign tours to be undertaken. In November 2022, The King welcomed the President of South Africa, Cyril Ramaphosa, for the first visit by a foreign head of state of his reign.

It was behind the scenes that the change of monarch was starting to be felt. The first issue to be resolved concerned the COP27 climate change conference in Egypt in November. The King had accepted an invitation to attend before his mother's passing, when Boris Johnson had been prime minister. The new Prime Minister Liz Truss felt it would not be appropriate for the

British monarch to attend and so she advised The King to now decline his invitation.

The King followed constitutional convention – despite his long involvement campaigning on climate change – and accepted his prime minister's advice but he did host a pre-conference reception at Buckingham Palace that brought together 200 business leaders, politicians, and campaigners. This allowed him to show his support for the aims of COP27, without overshadowing the British government's delegation to the event.

The King did not have to accept Liz Truss' advice for very long. On October 20, she resigned from office and became the shortest serving prime minister in British political history. Five days later her replacement, Rishi Sunak, arrived at Buckingham Palace to offer to form a government. As per the British unwritten constitution, The King formally accepted and held his first audience with his second prime minister in as many months.

Within the royal family, the passing of Queen Elizabeth II had prompted the start of a process of reorganisation that is still underway. The King had long had ambitions to slim down the royal 'firm' to a core group, centred around the new Prince and Princess of Wales, the Princess Royal and the Duke and Duchess of Edinburgh. This state of affairs was largely a result of the aging of several of the minor royals – the Dukes of Kent and Gloucester, and Princess Alexandra were all in their seventies or eighties and suffering from health issues – and Princes Andrew and Harry were no longer active members of the royal family.

With fewer working royals it was inevitable that a shake-up in how the royal family operated was essential. It became necessary to look again at all the charities and organisations Queen Elizabeth II supported, as well as her links to British and Commonwealth military units. This meant the new King would also have to look at the organisations he was affiliated to as Prince

The King laid the first wreath on the Cenotaph. (MOD/ Crown Copyright)

October was a month of high political drama in London with Prime Minister Liz Truss' fall from power after the shortest stay in Downing Street of any British political leader. (@RoyalFamily)

The King's first Christmas broadcast from the King George VI Memorial Chapel was well received and saw him pay tribute to his late mother. (@RoyalFamily)

The Prince of Wales and other members of the royal family were back on the road with the full programme of visits and engagements during the later weeks of 2022. Here he is visiting RAF Coningsby in Lincolnshire. (MOD/Crown Copyright)

The first images of The King to be released by Buckingham Palace in the days after Queen Elizabeth II's funeral showed the new monarch at work on his state papers and his famous 'red box' of government correspondence. (@RoyalFamily)

> **"My mother's belief in the power of that light was an essential part of her faith in God, but also her faith in people and it is one which I share with my whole heart,""**

of Wales.

These links had been built up over several decades and untangling or re-assigning them would be very complicated and require careful diplomacy. As many involved organisations in Commonwealth countries, there was an added level of sensitivity involved. To unpick and re-launch these affiliations, the royal household is conducting a review of royal patronages and as we go to press it is still unfolding.

Reorganising the royal family also involved some legal moves to allow new members to stand-in for The King during some state functions, including Privy Council meetings, royal visits, and the signing of some state papers. This involved the creation of new counsellors of state. The Queen Consort and Princess Beatrice became counsellors of state automatically as they moved up the line of succession with the passing of Queen Elizabeth II, to join Princes William, Harry, and Andrew.

On November 14, 2022, The King sent a message to both Houses of Parliament, formally asking for a change in the law that would allow the Princess Royal and Prince Edward to be added to the list of counsellors of state. The next day, a bill to that end was introduced in Parliament and it received royal assent on December 6, coming into force on December 7.

The first months of The King's reign were marked by numerous milestones as he took over many duties from his mother. One of the highest profile was his first Christmas broadcast to Britain and the Commonwealth, which was recorded in the Chapel of St George at Windsor Castle, where only a few weeks earlier Queen Elizabeth II had been laid to rest.

"I am reminded of the deeply touching letters, cards and messages which so many of you have sent my wife and myself and I cannot thank you enough for the love and sympathy you have shown our whole family," said The King. "Christmas is a particularly poignant time for all of us who have lost loved ones. We feel their absence at every familiar turn of the season and remember them in each cherished tradition.

"My mother's belief in the power of that light was an essential part of her faith in God, but also her faith in people and it is one which I share with my whole heart," he continued. "It

Despite having a new monarch, the National Service of Remembrance followed the traditional format, with thousands of veterans marching past the Cenotaph in Whitehall. (MOD/Crown Copyright)

is a belief in the extraordinary ability of each person to touch, with goodness and compassion, the lives of others, and to shine a light in the world around them. This is the essence of our community and the very foundation of our society.

"We see it in the selfless dedication of our armed forces and emergency services who work tirelessly to keep us all safe, and who performed so magnificently as we mourned the passing of our late Queen," he said. "We see it in our health and social care professionals, our teachers and indeed all those working in public service, whose skill and commitment are at the heart of our communities.

"And at this time of great anxiety and hardship, be it for those around the world facing conflict, famine or natural disaster, or for those at home finding ways to pay their bills and keep their families fed and warm, we see it in the humanity of people throughout our nations and the Commonwealth who so readily respond to the plight of others," he said. "I particularly want to pay tribute to all those wonderfully kind people who so generously give food or donations, or that most precious commodity of all, their time, to support those around them in greatest need, together with the many charitable organisations which do such extraordinary work in the most difficult circumstances. Our churches, synagogues, mosques, temples and gurdwaras, have once again united in feeding the hungry, providing love and support throughout the year. Such heartfelt solidarity is the most inspiring expression of loving our neighbour as our self.

"While Christmas is, of course, a Christian celebration, the power of light overcoming darkness is celebrated across the boundaries of faith and belief," he concluded. "So, whatever faith you have, or whether you have none, it is in this life-giving light, and with the true humility that lies in our service to others, that I believe we can find hope for the future." ●

THE KING MAKES HIS MARK

New Royal Insignia

Regimental standards, as well as other military badges and insignia, are not being immediately changed to incorporate King Charles III's new cypher on cost grounds. A rolling programme of renewal is underway and could take several years. (MOD/Crown Copyright)

The first memorial coins bearing King Charles III's image were struck in October 2022 ahead of the start of mass production of the first circulating coins for day-to-day use(Royal Mint)

All post from King Charles III is now franked with his cypher. (@RoyalFamily)

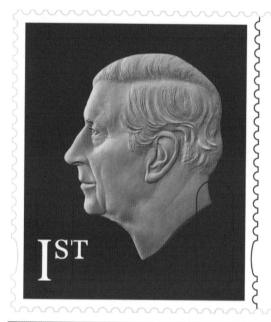

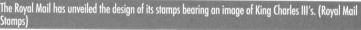

The Royal Mail has unveiled the design of its stamps bearing an image of King Charles III's. (Royal Mail Stamps)

King Charles III's new cypher was revealed on September 27, 2022, and will be replace the late Queen's cypher on all royal insignia. (@RoyalFamily)

The accession of a new monarch signals the start of huge exercise to rebrand official documents, insignia, regalia, uniforms, buildings, post boxes, stamps, coins, and bank notes.

Some of this - such as changing insignia on acts of parliament or government orders - takes places almost immediately to give them legal authority. In most other cases, such as the monarch's face on bank notes, the change is done over time to avoid unnecessary expense and work. Some things, such as replacing doors of post boxes, will probably never be changed.

The most important change is to the royal cypher, which typically consists of a monarch's name and title, sometimes interwoven with or surmounted by a crown. It changes with each reign and a new design is approved by the new monarch.

King Charles III's new cypher was revealed on September 27, 2022. It consists of the initials of his name, Charles, and title, Rex (Latin for King), alongside a representation of the Tudor crown. The Scottish version features the Crown of Scotland and was approved by Lord Lyon King of Arms.

The new King's cypher will appear on government buildings, state documents and on some post boxes. It will also be used by government departments and by the royal household for franking mail. On The King's orders the decision to replace cyphers will be at the discretion of individual organisations, and the process will be gradual.

Several police forces in England and Wales currently feature the royal cypher of Queen Elizabeth II in the centre of their helmet plates. These are also likely to be changed in due course.

Shortly after the beginning of a new reign, a new Great Seal of the Realm (used to authorise proclamations and other instruments) is presented to the lord chancellor during a meeting of the Privy Council. The old Great Seal is ritually defaced by the monarch. The same ceremony takes place for the Scottish Seal (often erroneously referred to as the 'Great Seal of Scotland'). A new Welsh Seal and Great Seal of Northern Ireland will also be commissioned. As per orders in council, approved at the Accession Council in September 2022, the old seals remain in use until replacements are ready.

All UK passports issued in the name of 'Her Majesty' remain valid for travel, but the wording on the inside of the front cover of new passports issued will likely be updated to 'His Britannic Majesty's Secretary of State Requests and requires in the Name of His Majesty all those whom it may concern to allow the bearer to pass freely without let or hindrance...'

The direction a monarch faces on coinage alternates with each reign. Custom also dictates that Latin be used for the title. The Royal Mint in Llantrisant, South Wales is gradually switching from circulating coins bearing Queen Elizabeth II's image to those carrying the new King's image. The first batch of 9.6m commemorative 50p coins entered circulation in December 2022. As with previous accessions, coinage bearing the image of the former sovereign will remain in circulation for several years as the transition takes place. This is a major project as some 27bn individual coins are believed by Royal Mail to be in circulation in Britain at any point in time.

Queen Elizabeth II appeared on all Bank of England notes after 1960. These will gradually be phased out and substituted with new designs featuring The King. The Bank of England has announced that bank notes bearing King Charles III's image will be ready to be issued from mid 2024. Notes issued by Scottish and Northern Irish banks did not depict the monarch so are not impacted.

Since 1967, all postage stamps issued by the Royal Mail have featured an embossed profile silhouette of Queen Elizabeth II. Although these can still be used on letters and parcels, the Royal Mail has commissioned new designs and new first and second class stamps are to be issued from April 4, 2023. ●

LOOKING FORWARD

A New King For a New Era

The King travelled to Salisbury Plain in February to visit Ukrainian soldiers training in Britain. (@Royal Family)

The first two weeks of 2023 were dominated by media coverage of Prince Harry's memoir, Spare. King Charles III, and other members of the royal family, made no public comments on the global media storm created by the book, which within a few weeks had sold more than four million copies worldwide.

It was business as usual at Buckingham Palace and royal visits continued as scheduled. The King did not appear to be interested in participating in a Twitter spat with his son and daughter-in-law. He had his own agenda and was not going to be diverted. This suggests he has a long term plan for his reign that goes beyond ring mastering family fallouts.

The King has long had an interest in climate change and other environmental issues, as well as pursing social justice. Although as monarch he is constitutionally constrained in making overtly political statements or high profile visits to controversial locations there is no sign that King Charles III is ready to lead a quiet life. He appears keen to use all the levers at his disposal to set an example for others to follow or to bring key decision makers together. The jargon phrase is making use of the 'power to convene'.

He was advised by the then Prime Minister Liz Truss that as King he should no longer attend the COP26 climate change summit in Egypt. He, however, was able to host many of the key figures involved in the summit at a reception at Buckingham Palace in the run-up to the event.

Perhaps the most striking example of The King using his power to set an example took place on January 19, 2023, when the Crown Estates, which controls royal-owned land around the United Kingdom and off its shores, announced that it would re-direct £1bn in profits from several new off shore wind farm developments to be given to HM Treasury. This would be

Prince Harry's memoir was a global best seller in January 2023. (Philafrenzy)

The King has diverted profits from the Crown Estates' extensive interests in off shore wind farms to the public good. (Hans Hillewaert)

The new Prince and Princess of Wales were quick to visit the principality to link up with charities and good causes. (Kensington Palace)

"The monarch surrenders the revenue from the estate – more than £312m a year – to the HM Treasury each year for the benefit of the nation's finances"

used for the 'wider public good' by the British government. Under the Sovereign Grant Act of 2011, the royal family is funded via a percentage of Crown Estates profits, so any increase in its revenue would have normally generated an increase in the royal family's annual revenue but, The King's move kept the royal family's income flat.

The Crown Estate – an ancient portfolio of land and property – belongs to the reigning monarch 'in right of the crown' but it is not their private property.

The monarch surrenders the revenue from the estate – more than £312m a year – to the HM

Treasury each year for the benefit of the nation's finances, in exchange for the Sovereign Grant. The King receives 25% of the Crown Estate's annual surplus, which is currently just over £86m a year, and includes an extra 10% for the refurbishment of Buckingham Palace.

A Buckingham Palace spokesperson said: "In view of the offshore energy windfall, the keeper of the privy purse has written to the prime minister and the chancellor of the exchequer to share The King's wish that this windfall be directed for wider public good, rather than to the Sovereign Grant, through an appropriate reduction in the proportion of Crown Estate ➲

On February 8, 2023, King Charles III hosted the embattled President of Ukraine, Volodymyr Zelensky, to Buckingham Palace during his first visit to Britain since the Russian invasion of his country. @Royal Family)

surplus that funds the sovereign grant."

The new lease agreement is for six offshore wind projects that have the potential to power more than seven million homes. Three of the six projects are located off the north Wales, Cumbrian, and Lancashire coast, and three are located in the North Sea off the Yorkshire and Lincolnshire coast. Together they will pay about £1bn to the Crown Estate every year.

The Crown Estates own almost all of the sea bed around the British Isles from the mean low water mark out to the 12 mile limit of British sovereign territorial waters. The January 2023 award of leases for wind farms is the fourth made by the Crown Estates and will bring the amount of power generated by off shore wind farms covered by its leases to 41 gigawatts, which could potentially power 41% of British homes. The British government has set a target of generating 500 gigawatts from off shore wind farms by 2030. In addition to this, Crown Estate research has indicated the economic potential to accommodate up to an additional 20 gigawatts of offshore wind capacity by 2045.

> **"The King is working to ensure that the nations of the United Kingdom remain united or at least remain on good terms."**

This move pushed many buttons for The King. He was contributing in a material way to moving Britain toward its net zero objective of transitioning to generating all its electricity from renewable resources. By declining to accept the windfall profit from the future wind farm developments The King was also making a statement about responsible business practices, at a time when many energy companies were reporting multi-billion pound growth in profits.

King Charles III had famously undertaken the 'longest royal apprenticeship' in British history but since his accession to the throne he has shown that he is keen to adapt and modernise the royal family and its place in British life. Former Prime Minister Tony Blair famously coined the phrase, "Britain should be a force for good", and King Charles III appears to want to follow in the tradition.

In his own way, The King is working to ensure that the nations of the United Kingdom remain united or at least remain on good terms. His visits to the capitals of Scotland, Northern Ireland, and Wales in the run up to Queen Elizabeth II's funeral were a clear effort to show that he respected the devolved assemblies and their elected governments. Treating them as equal partners in the United Kingdom was a pointed statement that some politicians in London might not have agreed with.

For a man of 75 years, The King appears in robust good health - like his mother and father before him - meaning he could reign for two more decades if their longevity is any guide. Britain's active monarch looks like he will be working as a "force for good" for many years to come. ●